C000310978

Towards the Compassionate School

Bringing compassion into education and learning

Towards the Compassionate School

From golden rule to golden thread

Edited by Maurice Irfan Coles

A Trentham Book
Institute of Education Press

First published in 2015 by the UCL Institute of Education Press, University College London, 20 Bedford Way, London WC1H 0AL

ioepress.co.uk

© Maurice Coles 2015

British Library Cataloguing in Publication Data:
A catalogue record for this publication is available from the British Library

ISBNs
978-1-85856-526-2 (paperback)
978-1-85856-527-9 (PDF eBook)
978-1-85856-528-6 (ePub eBook)
978-1-85856-529-3 (Kindle eBook)

All rights reserved. No part of this publication may be reproduced, stored in a retrieval system, or transmitted in any form or by any means, electronic, mechanical, photocopying, recording or otherwise, without the prior permission of the copyright owner.

Every effort has been made to trace copyright holders and to obtain their permission for the use of copyright material. The publisher apologizes for any errors or omissions and would be grateful if notified of any corrections that should be incorporated in future reprints or editions of this book.

The opinions expressed in this publication are those of the authors and do not necessarily reflect the views of the UCL Institute of Education, University College London.

Typeset by Quadrant Infotech (India) Pvt Ltd
Printed by CPI Group (UK) Ltd, Croydon, CR0 4YY
Cover image ©Monkey Business Images/Shutterstock.com

All proceeds from the sale of the book by the CoED Foundation will go towards supporting the Foundation's work.

Contents

List of figures

List of abbreviations

ASDAN	Award Scheme Development and Accreditation Network
CCARE	Center for Compassion and Altruism Research and Education
CFT	compassion-focused therapy
CoPE	Certificate of Personal Effectiveness
CPD	continuing professional development
CRC	Convention on the Rights of the Child
DfE	Department for Education
DfES	Department for Education and Skills
EBI	Even Better If
FRSA	Fellow Royal Society of Arts
GCSE	General Certificate of Secondary Education
GPIW	Global Peace Initiative of Women
HTI	Heads, Teachers and Industry
IHPE	Institute of Health Promotion and Education
IMF	International Monetary Fund
LEA	local education authority
MBCT	mindfulness-based cognitive therapy
MBSR	mindfulness-based stress reduction
MiSP	Mindfulness in Schools Project
MSC	Mindful Self-Compassion
MT	Mindfulness Training
NACCCE	National Advisory Committee on Creative and Cultural Education
NICE	National Institute for Health and Care Excellence
NICEN	National and International Compassion in Education Network
NVC	non-violent communication
OECD	Organisation for Economic Co-operation and Development
Ofsted	Office for Standards in Education, Children's Services and Skills
PHE	Public Health England
PISA	Programme for International Student Assessment

PSHE	personal, social, health and economic education
QCA	Qualifications and Curriculum Authority
RACA	Raising African Caribbean Achievement
RAK	Random Acts of Kindness
RoSPA	The Royal Society for the Prevention of Accidents
RSA	Royal Society of Arts
SCAA	School Curriculum and Assessment Authority
SDSA	School Development Support Agency
SEAL	Social and Emotional Aspects of Learning
SEL	Social and Emotional Learning
SMSC	spiritual, moral, social and cultural development
UNICEF	United Nations Children's Fund

Foreword

Just over 50 years ago, Martin Luther King, Jr, while facing a lack of compassion for his right to social justice in the American south, maintained his stance of justice, peace and love, for which he was later awarded the Nobel Peace Prize. When Dr King departed the United States for Oslo, Norway, on 4 December 1964, he stopped in London for three days to preach at St Paul's Cathedral and meet with leaders of the peace community. Days later, on 10 December, King accepted the prize (King, 1964a) in the name of the thousands of people in the civil rights movement who constituted what he termed a 'mighty army of love'.

When presenting the Nobel Peace Prize to King, Gunnar Jahn, chairman of the Nobel Committee, praised him for being 'the first person in the Western world to have shown us that a struggle can be waged without violence'. Jahn went on to say that, 'He is the first to make the message of brotherly love a reality in the course of his struggle, and he has brought this message to all men, to all nations and races.'

King's message of love and compassion embodies the Golden Rule: *Treat others as you would wish to be treated.* His compassionate sensibility led him to focus not only on the soul of the individual but also on the holistic well-being of the entire person – mind, body and spirit. The dichotomy between the sacred and the secular in his theology moved him beyond being simply a civil rights leader for America and catapulted him onto the world stage as an international human rights leader who brought a resounding message of compassion, love and hope that change could come for the oppressed. His God enabled him to see the interrelatedness of all humankind. In *Strength to Love* (1963), he wrote:

> In a real sense, all life is interrelated. All men are caught in an inescapable network of mutuality, tied in a single garment of destiny. Whatever affects one directly affects all indirectly. I can never be what I ought to be until you are what you ought to be, and you can never be what you ought to be until I'm what I ought to be. This is the interrelated structure of reality.

In the pages of this book we find interrelated concepts, theories and practical overviews for an education system delivered through a vision of compassionate schools. One of the most misused phases in organizational development is the ideology that 'where there is no vision the people perish'. It is misused, because people cannot differentiate a vision from a mirage. A mirage is an illusion. It appears to be grounded in reality but when you seek to put your hands on it, you find it has no substance. It is fool's gold and when you get it you find out very quickly that all that glitters is not gold.

A true vision, on the other hand, is an inspired perspective on the world as it should be. Its reality is grounded outside self-will and ambition. It promotes the best in the human spirit and its end is to create a beloved community. A true vision for compassionate schools is realized when civic, political and religious leaders come together to ensure all children and families, regardless of ethnicity, race, socioeconomic status, are equipped for academic success: that is not a mirage, but a vision.

The need for compassionate schools binds us first in fidelity. And understanding that fidelity is the reality that every individual has value and that those values are rooted in their culture. Education has been a cultural value of all people since the beginning of time. All have sought academic excellence, through various mediums of learning. Through education, we bring our creative energies to bear on improving the quality of life.

Equally important is fellowship. Fellowship enhances families and creates positive space for human interaction. The quest for all humanity is to seek a place of peace. A place, if you will, where the lion lays down with the lamb. There is something in the human spirit that seeks solitude, serenity and safety.

Also, it is the right of every person to acquire the skills needed to function effectively in our society. Everyone, however different, has the capacity to be an educated functional member of the world, provided the right resources are made available. These are the ideas we must be dedicated to: fidelity to every child's cultural value; fellowship that creates every child's community; and furthering of programmes and resources that prove the functionality of every child's well-being. These basic concepts are the ideal for a compassionate education system and compassionate schools.

Martin Luther King Jr argued that to focus narrowly on matters of private morality while ignoring the moral implications of our public policy was a misnomer. In 'A Might Army of Love', he further lamented that:

> One of the great tragedies of life is that men seldom bridge the gulf between practice and profession, between doing and saying. A persistent schizophrenia leaves so many of us tragically divided against ourselves. ... How often are our lives characterized by a high blood pressure of creeds and anaemia of deeds! We talk

eloquently about our commitment to the principles of Christianity, and yet our lives are saturated with the practices of paganism. We proclaim our devotion to democracy, but we sadly practice the opposite of the democratic creed. We talk passionately about peace, and at the same time we assiduously prepare for war. We make our fervent pleas for the high road of justice, and then we tread unflinchingly the low road of injustice. This strange dichotomy, this agonizing gulf between the ought and the is, represents the tragic theme of man's earthly pilgrimage.

In *Towards the Compassionate School: From Golden Rule to Golden Thread*, we awaken private thoughts to take on a public stance for our children. In all children we should discover their value. We all have a responsibility to love and care for the entire well-being of all of the children of the world. That is compassion.

Dr Keith Magee, Visiting Scholar and Director, Social Justice Institute, Boston University, and Honorary Distinguished Senior Fellow, University of Birmingham

Preface

It did not matter what religion you were, what faith you believed in ... it was life, it was survival, it was the future ... it represents the human spirit ... it represents good over evil ... it represents how people will care for each other at the worst time and moment in their life. And how people can put aside their differences for the greater good.

(Richard Sheirer, New York Commissioner of
Emergency Management, writing about the World Trade Center
Cross at Ground Zero, 9/11 Memorial Museum)

It has perhaps more to do with synchronicity than accident that I wrote this preface in a public library in New York after an amazing two-week sojourn in the United States that had taken me to Compassion Week in San Francisco, two incredibly compassionate schools – Tara Redwood in California and Epiphany in Boston, MA – a number of compassionate speaking engagements in Boston, and, finally, the 9/11 Memorial Museum in downtown New York. The memorial and museum, although harrowing in relating the events of the day that changed America, truly represent the victory of the compassionate spirit in its ability to overcome even the greatest evils.

Work in this library also represents the end of the first part of the history of the CoED Foundation, a non-profit charity based in England, established in 2012 and dedicated to bringing compassion into education and learning. It signals the near completion of this book, the fruit of two years' work by nine contributors in three continents, and the first of a number of planned writings and projects that the Foundation hopes to accomplish. The Foundation did not begin its life with a major focus on compassion – its name was devised from its original primary purposes (which remain its charitable objectives in English law), with the 'Co' being for the promotion of Cohesion, the E for Equality and the D for Diversity. It was Rehana Mughal, one of the Foundation's Trustees and Advisory Board (TAB) members, who kept pressing me as we sat in London's British Library, continually asking 'What is it about?' 'What is it really about?' until, in a moment of gestalt, I replied, 'You can sum it up in one word – compassion. It is about bringing compassion into education and learning.'

That word 'compassion' not only resonated fully with the TAB, who have supported the work from the outset, but also struck a chord with our patrons and associates who are drawn from a wide range of backgrounds in the United States, Britain and elsewhere. It rings true wherever I go in the world, with people saying, 'Compassion in education; what a wonderful idea!' The fact that it appears novel, rather than as it is – a twenty-first-century reworking of the wisdom of the ancients – is a sad indictment of what education has become, at least in the so-called 'developed' world. So now we have very active associates in Canada, the United States and Austria, and a number of interested parties who are waiting to act in Pakistan, Argentina and Australia. When the Foundation enjoyed its formal launch at the Houses of Parliament in March 2014, one of our patrons and sponsors, Estelle Morris, Baroness of Yardley (former Secretary of State for Education in the Blair government's first term), argued that the key to the Foundation's success would be what impact it had internationally. Having a compassionate English education system is a noble aim but one that could easily be undermined in a world of indifference and hostility.

Taking that small step towards a compassionate education system led us to become an international partner organization for the Charter for Compassion; to be expert witnesses in the Royal Society of Arts (RSA) research 'Schools with Soul' (Peterson *et al.*, 2014); and to a series of speaking engagements in Boston University and Wheelock College, engineered by our American patron, Dr Keith McGee. Like most charitable non-profitable organizations, we struggle for money, and in such difficult times we may always have that burden but, hopefully, our influence will far outweigh our size and penury.

This preface marks the end of the first stage of the Foundation's journey but also marks another milestone in my personal journey, which has privileged me with over 45 years in a range of capacities in the English education system, travel to over one-third of the world's countries, and a close relationship with three of the world's major faith traditions. For me, the CoED Foundation marks the blessed zenith of an educational voyage characterized by a lifetime's advocacy of race and faith equality, of diversity and cohesion.

Most of all, however, I have been greatly blessed with Nina, my long-suffering British-born Indian wife, and my daughters, Lara and Rohesia, all of whom have allowed me the space and shared the vision and some of the burdens throughout. It is always difficult to name individuals who have been so supportive for fear of upsetting somebody you have omitted. But, in the certain and apologetic knowledge that this will happen, I need to call out several key names for thanks and praise. The Foundation's chairman and vice-chairman, Professors David Woods and Mick Waters, both contributors to this book, have been unstinting in their support and patience from the outset. All members of the Trustees and Advisory Board have contributed enormously to this work but I must mention Dr Bill Gent, who has painstakingly gone through every line of the drafts and commented most helpfully. Khalid Mahmood of the School Development Support Agency (SDSA) has soothed my fevered woes and smoothed out my many IT and formatting issues. Throughout, my friend 'since morning' Pastor Gilroy Brown has offered spiritual succour; and my new friend Dr Keith McGee has ensured we will capture the United States at the highest levels of government. Dr John Lloyd and Dr Tamara Russell have been fantastic, both in the completion of their chapters and in their level of general support. Rabiyah Latif and Tas Bashir have provided the creative flair so lacking in this editor.

Much of my thinking has been deeply influenced by the work of the Empathy and Compassion in Society conferences, and by Llewellyn Vaughan-Lee of the Golden Sufi Center. Last, but not least, I cannot praise highly enough Gillian Klein, our friend, supporter and Senior Fellow in Publishing of Trentham Books at IOE Press, who has kept faith and supported us from the outset. Finally, all praise is due to 'Him who has no name, and comes by whatever name you call him', without whom this journey would not have happened, and to whom ultimately everything is owed.

Maurice Irfan Coles
St Agnes New York Public Library, 444 Amsterdam Avenue, New York, November 2014

About the contributors

Gilroy Brown, Associate and member of the Trustees and Advisory Board, CoED Foundation

Gilroy served for 37 years in the education service, including 10 years as Headteacher of an inner-city, multicultural school and 11 years as a School Adviser in Birmingham local authority's Primary Leadership and Management Team. He delivers bespoke Leadership and Management training for school leaders, including the Local Induction Programme for new heads via the National College for Leadership.

Gilroy led two research projects on raising African-Caribbean achievement in schools (RACA), which were published as models for best practice. He has delivered a comprehensive training programme for local authority advisers to develop their knowledge and skills to support schools in raising the attainment of African-Caribbean pupils. He worked in the team of national consultants commissioned by the Department for Education and Skills (DfES) that led on the Aiming High programmes that significantly improved black students' attainment in both primary and secondary schools.

Maurice Irfan Coles, CEO, CoED Foundation

Maurice has worked in education's public and private sectors for 45 years. He was a teacher in London, then a Staff Inspector in Birmingham specializing in anti-racist education. Over a period of 18 years, he held eight portfolios and led two large support services. A registered Ofsted inspector in all school sectors, he was the first CEO of the School Development Support Agency (SDSA), a social enterprise based in Leicester City. In 2012, he founded the CoED Foundation, a charity dedicated to bringing compassion into education and learning.

Maurice has led on a number of collaborative projects, including the internationally acclaimed Islam and Citizenship Education Project, Curriculum Enrichment for the Common Era, a company dedicated to producing heritage materials, and the Sacred Spaces Project. He has written extensively on school improvement, race equality, intercultural education and continuing professional development (CPD). His books are *Faith, Interfaith and Cohesion: The Education Dimension* and *Every Muslim Child Matters*. His report, *Mending Broken Britain: Education's Response*, provides causal analysis and recommendations concerning the UK riots of summer 2011. From a Christian background and with a Hindu wife and mixed-heritage daughters, Maurice has converted to Islam.

Dr John Lloyd, Associate, CoED Foundation

John is the President of the Institute of Health Promotion and Education (IHPE), having been Policy Adviser for the PSHE Association. He was Adviser for PSHE and Citizenship Education at the Department for Children, Schools and Families (DCSF), after working as a Senior Adviser in Birmingham Advisory and Support Service. A member of the PSHE Advisory Group and Citizenship Working Party, he contributed to the development of both the PSHE Framework and the statutory citizenship curriculum in England. He is co-author of *Democracy Then and Now* and *Blueprints for Health Education*, and co-editor of the *Health Promoting Primary School*, among other publications. John was Adviser to Channel 4's *Schools All About Us* television series, of which *No Bullying Here* and *Karl's Story* won the Royal Television Society Gold Award. A contributor to the QCA Citizenship Schemes of Work and the revised Citizenship and PSHE programmes of study in 2007, he chaired the Personal Development Reference Group at the QCA. John is a member of RoSPA's National Risk and Safety Education Committee, a member of the IHPE Board and a Trustee of the University of the First Age, the Alcohol Education Trust and Teachers in Development Education (Birmingham).

Revd Keith L. Magee, ThD, FRSA, Patron, CoED Foundation

The Reverend Keith Magee is an honorary senior research fellow on race, religion and poverty at the University of Birmingham Institute of Advance Studies and a visiting scholar at Boston University School of Theology. He also serves as senior pastor at Berachah Church, Boston, MA. His work is interwoven with his commitment to social justice and the cause of the poor. He works with universities, museums and non-governmental organizations to illuminate and interrupt the cycle of global poverty through scholarship, arts and culture. Keith trained at Harvard Divinity School, and brings both academic and practical knowledge, having served in various roles as non-profit executive, social historian, pastor of two inner-city congregations, and as a Senior Adviser to President Obama's campaign and the African American Clergy Network. In 2014, he was project director of the Yale Center for Dyslexia and Creativity's Multicultural Dyslexia Awareness Initiative, leading the charge on 'Dyslexia and the Achievement Gap: A Civil Rights Issue of Our Time'.

Dr Tamara Russell, MSc, PhD, DClinPsych, Associate, CoED Foundation

Tamara is Director of the Mindfulness Centre of Excellence in London, and Visiting Lecturer at King's College London. The Centre is dedicated to leading innovation and thought in the field of mindfulness, with a focus on creativity and thriving. She works as a mindfulness consultant and trainer in settings including education and health worldwide.

As a clinical psychologist, martial artist and neuroscientist, Tamara brings a unique, multi-layered perspective to her mindfulness teaching, therapy and research. The embodiment of mindfulness lies at the heart of her training programmes for schools, corporations, the health sector and the general public: 'The Art of Mindfulness' and 'Body in Mind Training'. Her academic research and her forthcoming book *Mindfullness in Motion* explore the link between movement, mind and the brain. Working with contemporary dancers and creative artists, she explores how we can learn and share experiences of embodiment across disciplines to improve the pedagogy of mindfulness.

Tiago P. Tatton-Ramos

Tiago P. Tatton-Ramos is a clinical psychologist and a PhD candidate at Universidade Federal do Rio Grande do Sul, Brazil, working on a body-based mindfulness intervention trial with ischemic heart disease patients. He is a member of the Experimental Phenomenology and Cognition Lab (LaFEC-UFRGS/RS) and one of the founding members of Iniciativa Mindfulness, a leading group of mindfulness research and practices in Brazil. He holds a visiting academic CAPES award to work in partnership with Tamara Russell at the Institute of Psychiatry, King's College London.

Professor Mick Waters, Vice Chair, CoED Foundation

Mick works with schools in the Black Country Challenge on raising standards in the West Midlands, and with schools across the country on innovative approaches to learning. He is an Honorary Fellow of the College of Teachers. He is patron of Heads, Teachers and Industry (HTI), of the Values Trust and of the Curriculum Foundation, which seeks to promote a voice for the power and potential of the whole curriculum.

Mick was Director of Curriculum at the QCA and, before that, Chief Education Officer for the City of Manchester. Key agendas included the development of joined-up children's services, the 14–19 strategy, the employment and skills dimension, and configuring all this around the Building Schools for the Future programme. Previously, Mick worked in Birmingham local education authority, where he drove forward a school improvement agenda that saw increasing achievements and schools reaching new levels in educational development. He has experience of headship in two schools and of working in teacher training. He has written books on the curriculum, teaching and learning, and management, as well as making presentations at numerous national and international conferences. Mick's latest book is *Thinking Allowed … on Schooling*.

Professor David Woods, CBE, Chair of Trustees, CoED Foundation

David has spent 20 years of his career in teaching, senior leadership in schools and in teacher training. He has worked in local authorities in Solihull and Birmingham, and became the Chief Education Adviser for Birmingham City, where he worked closely with Tim Brighouse. In 1998, he joined the Standards and Effectiveness Unit at the Department for Education and Skills (DfES) as Senior Education Adviser, working closely with Ministers to develop educational policy, and subsequently became the Head of the DfES Advisory Service.

He joined the London Challenge programme in 2003 as the Lead Secondary Adviser and became the Principal Adviser for the City Challenge, a role that was later extended across England, and in 2009 became Chief Adviser for London Schools. He is a member of the Ofsted Expert Panel on urban education and also of the National College's Steering Groups on Teaching Schools and NLEs. He is Visiting Professor of Education at

Maurice Irfan Coles

Warwick University and UCL Institute of Education. David has written and spoken extensively on school improvement and has co-authored books with Tim Brighouse on school improvement, including *What Makes a Good School Now?* and *The A–Z of School Improvement*.

Introduction
Maurice Irfan Coles

> *Now bless thyself: thou met'st with things dying. I with things new born.*
>
> (Shakespeare, *The Winter's Tale*)

This is a book of signposts, not simple solutions; of pathways, not prescriptions. This is a book that fundamentally argues that, unless we change the story of individualism and consumerism that we have bought into for so long, future generations will face almost insurmountable problems. This is a book that empirically, scientifically, morally and spiritually demonstrates that making compassion *the* key organizing principle of education and other systems *everywhere*, offers hope. This book aims to be visionary and mundane, inspirational and routine, providing the big-picture imperatives for change as well as practical suggestions for bringing them into being. It is based upon the humblest of all premises: compassion, defined as love in action, provides the meta value that, through the conscious implementation of the Golden Rule (treat others as you would wish to be treated), presents the simplest of operational yardsticks by which schools and society can measure themselves. The book aims to help readers realize that, to quote Einstein, 'We can't solve problems by using the same kind of thinking we used when we created them.' It aims to help readers see the world through the prism of compassion, to realize that compassion is a consciousness, a perspective that should permeate everything we do in education; should become our Golden Thread that weaves together curriculum, pedagogy and behaviours.

By the time students finish their statutory education, what do we hope they will have become? That is the question. Most of us would agree that we hope they would be fluent, decent, self-driven attainers who lived the democratic ideals to which we subscribe; that they would be compassionate individuals who cared for each other and cared for the planet. Few would argue with that and most in the education profession would maintain that it was what they were striving for.

The teaching profession has always been populated by some of the most compassionate people on the planet. You could not survive in the contemporary educational world – and sadly many young teachers do not – unless you had an overriding love for your students and for teaching and learning. You would not work the impossibly long hours, often in difficult circumstances. Many schools would argue that they are already compassionate institutions and that liberal education has had the whole child at its heart from at least as far back as the Greeks. So why at this juncture in our history is so much being written and said about creating compassionate schooling, compassionate cultures, compassionate organizations and compassionate societies? What are the strategic imperatives for change? If the ideas outlined in this book were implemented, what might the difference be in student behaviour and well-being? What is it about compassion that we actually want to see in schools?

The seven authors involved in *Towards the Compassionate School* have done their best to answers these questions in some detail; but the reality is that each chapter could form a book in itself. The authors have had to exercise great discipline in rendering many complex concepts simply and succinctly. Similar discipline was required to ensure the book did not become a political polemic against ideologies that are incompatible with the world view we share. Although some of the examples and the context are drawn from the English education system, the underlying principles and their application are totally universal and apply anywhere from Cambridge (England and Massachusetts) to Cairo, to the Cape.

How to use this book

The audience for this book is purposefully wide. It is written so that the general reader can grasp the rationale for creating a more compassionate society. Education policy-makers, and those responsible for moulding education, require the systemic overview and signposts for change. Teachers and all those who work in schools want some idea of what works and what they can try. This introduction provides a succinct overview and the conclusion reinforces the main points. Each chapter begins with a short abstract, which gives a flavour of what follows. The key points or take-home messages of each chapter are summarized on the CoED website (www.coedfoundation.org.uk). You may want to skim-read the first chapter because it unpacks compassion, with its coat of many colours, and explains the imperatives for change. The comprehensive index offers sharper focus. How you use it depends in part upon what you seek.

Although each author, including those who penned the Foreword and Afterword, wrote independently, all shared one aim, sought one overriding goal, perhaps best expressed in the words of His Holiness, the Dalai Lama (2012: Part 2):

My hope is that, one day, formal education will pay attention to what I call education of the heart. Just as we take for granted the need to acquire proficiency in the basic academic subjects, I am hopeful that a time will come when we can take it for granted that children will learn, as part of their school curriculum, the indispensability of inner values such as love, compassion, justice and forgiveness.

Chapter 1

Changing the story, altering the paradigm
Maurice Irfan Coles

Abstract

This chapter aims to provide the justification for making global compassion the key and fundamental organizing principle in *all* education systems. It sets out to demonstrate that, unless we embark on this course of action, unless we change the contemporary narrative, the future for our children and grandchildren looks very bleak indeed. Divided into three parts, the first summarizes the ten 'self-evident truths' that form the basic premises upon which the book is based. It defines terms like 'compassion', 'empathy' and 'altruism', and charts a way through this linguistic maze. The second examines in finer detail the self-evident truths that are the compassionate drivers; the imperatives for societal and educational change. The final part examines some of the educational implications of changing the narrative and altering the paradigm. It proffers some existing examples and provides pathways for change.

Part 1: Conceptions and misconceptions

Ten self-evident truths

It was the genius of American marketing and the glory of America's Founding Fathers that they elevated key democratic ideals to statements of 'self-evident truths' (1776) for, in reality, they were evident only to a few and true to even fewer. Our self-evident truths are far more prosaic. They are simply ten key statements that are empirically verifiable, that can – with the exception of the last aspirational 'truth' – be justified through evidential data and research. Our truths form the basic premises upon which this book is based. The brilliance of the Founding Fathers was that they constructed a binding story, a narrative upon which they built a nation and for which subsequent generations have been prepared to die.

We hold these truths to be self-evident:

i.	**That we are all wired for compassion**
ii.	**That the Golden Rule, treat others (and the Earth) as you would wish to be treated, is central to the world's ethical and religious traditions**
iii.	**That compassion is essential for good mental and physical health**
iv.	**That successful organizations are built upon compassionate values**
v.	**That technology has the power to become a key vehicle for spreading compassion**
vi.	**That many of the world's cities are places of super-diversity**
vii.	**That man-made climate change, and the evils of terror and counter-terror, have the potential to undermine the forces of compassion**
viii.	**That our present economic system does not encourage compassion**
ix.	**That compassion can be taught, caught and cultivated**
x.	**That compassion can become education's key unifying meta-value; its central organizing principle**

Figure 1.1: Ten self-evident truths

Every nation has a story that binds it together, a dominant narrative that encapsulates what it stands for, what it believes in. The story is significant because it underpins the paradigms, the sets of practices and thought-patterns that give meaning to people's lives. The dominant story of the West, in living memory, has been individualism and consumerism, so much so that these are now the accepted norms. This story is under increasing challenge, however, partly because growth at the expense of the planet is unsustainable, and partly because it fails to provide human beings with any deep sense of meaning in their lives, any real satisfying purpose. As Llewellyn Vaughan-Lee (2013a) puts it, 'We long for a story that can give meaning to our daily lives and restore the health and beauty of the planet, but we remain caught in our tale of celebrating stuff.' His conclusion is straightforward: 'The only way to change the world is to change the story.'

Education is not immune from this narrative For many, the purpose of education is to provide better access to this consumerist dream. You go to school to pass exams, to get a better job and to get more money!

Governments strive to achieve a world-class education system, as measured by the Organisation for Economic Co-operation and Development (OECD) with its Programme for International Student Assessment (PISA), which has come 'to rule the world' (Stewart, 2013). The problem is that PISA offers a very narrow comparative attainment-based model, assessing maths, reading, science and computer-based problem-solving. Perhaps unsurprisingly for an organization dedicated to economic cooperation, it does not assess the many other skills and attitudes required by twenty-first-century students. In response to their international league table position, however, governments allocate resources and change systems, desperately trying to climb PISA's 'greasy pole'.

High attainment is important for attaining success in later life but any system that lauds academic attainment at the expense of all else – assesses it, inspects it and places the results in public league tables – lacks balance. We now have the brightest students and the best teachers the world has ever known but, as Harry R. Lewis, former Dean of Harvard, puts it, we have produced 'excellence without a soul' (2006). For Lewis, this excellence is 'hollow', because higher education (and, by implication, those lower down the educational food chain) has forgotten its essential purpose of creating better, well-rounded, moral individuals. Lewis is unequivocal as to cause: 'Two main forces combine to produce these troubling circumstances – competition and consumerism' (7).

He is equally clear about the solution. Harvard's leaders have to embody self-understanding, strength of character, 'compassion and empathy for others, as well as scholarly excellence' (266). Compassion and compassionate education can provide a new story from which we can evolve new paradigms. Compassion may be a story as old as time, but now it needs to be restored to the heart of education and learning.

So what is compassion? Compassion is related to a large cluster of descriptors expressing human behaviours, emotions and attitudes. Google 'compassion' and you will find over 30 synonyms and related words, many stressing love. Google 'love' and you have over 20 descriptors. Defining love in English has always been problematic because the one word encompasses divine, 'brotherly', parental and romantic love, some of them active states and some passive. Compassion, however, is less nuanced and shares a linguistic oneness with many other languages, irrespective of historical time and context. In English, the word derives from the Latin *compati*, which literally means to *suffer with*, implying that it involves more than one person: that it is relational. In addition, it also implies that suffering is accompanied by action to alleviate its causes. As Archbishop Desmond Tutu put it:

Compassion is not just feeling with someone, but seeking to change the situation. Frequently people think compassion and love are merely sentimental. No! They are very demanding. If you are going to be compassionate be prepared for action.'

(cited in Chang, 2006: 139)

The word has the same dual meaning in Greek (*symponia*), in Arabic (*rahma*), in Hebrew (*rachamim*), in Sanskrit and Pali (*karuna)* and in Punjabi (*daya*). Put simply: compassion is love in action. It is a gentle word but a radical concept because it demands change.

Scholars in various disciplines have offered a number of more detailed definitions but there is overall agreement that there are three components to compassion:

a) the recognition of a person's or a group's suffering

b) an empathetic response to that suffering

c) an active determination to alleviate the distress and, where possible, the causes of that distress.

The depth of our response and the capacity of our attempts to overcome suffering are often related to context. Thus, we tend to feel more deeply and respond more quickly if the sufferer is known to us, like a member of our family, a close friend or near neighbour. Paul Ekman, one of the world's foremost experts on emotions, refers to this as 'proximal compassion', which he distinguishes from 'distal compassion', involving acting now in order to avoid future pain and anguish. The best example of distal compassion, and most difficult to secure agreement on, is action to avoid climate disaster. This, Ekman powerfully argues, requires 'global compassion', which, for him, is 'a concern to alleviate the suffering of anyone, regardless of their nationality, language, culture or religion' (2014: 13).

Educationalists, like all those in the caring professions, would probably argue that global compassion is one of their aims, and, hopefully, is part of their practice. To become more meaningful in the school curriculum, however, a taxonomy of compassion is required, one that is broken down into more detailed descriptors, which can then act as school-based objectives that will determine the school's values, attitudes and behavioural standards. The CoED Foundation brainstormed the potential qualities of a compassionate human being which, remarkably, were transformed into a simple but telling mnemonic, 'acts for love'. Its descriptors can be seen both as active verbs, describing compassionate motivational behaviours, and as adjectives, outlining the characteristics of compassionate human beings. These qualities are aspirational, a series of 'mights'. The range of possible characteristics will vary in degree according to individual personality, culture and context of time, but they do contain the essential principles of acting compassionately.

Acts for love

A COMPASSIONATE HUMAN BEING MIGHT BE ...

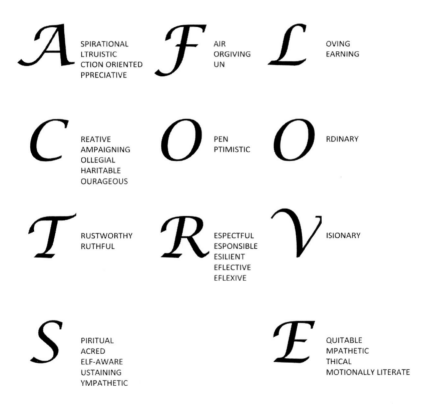

A
SPIRATIONAL
LTRUISTIC
CTION ORIENTED
PPRECIATIVE

F
AIR
ORGIVING
UN

L
OVING
EARNING

C
REATIVE
AMPAIGNING
OLLEGIAL
HARITABLE
OURAGEOUS

O
PEN
PTIMISTIC

O
RDINARY

T
RUSTWORTHY
RUTHFUL

R
ESPECTFUL
ESPONSIBLE
ESILIENT
EFLECTIVE
EFLEXIVE

V
ISIONARY

S
PIRITUAL
ACRED
ELF-AWARE
USTAINING
YMPATHETIC

E
QUITABLE
MPATHETIC
THICAL
MOTIONALLY LITERATE

COMPASSION IS LOVE IN ACTION

Figure 1.2: Acts for love

Some of these characteristics are self-explanatory; others require further clarification, especially when applied to the field of education.

Altruistic

An altruistic person operates on the basis of selflessness, of kindness to others, with no desire for personal reward or praise. Altruism is a traditional virtue in many cultures, and is central to most religious traditions and secular worldviews. The opposite of selfishness, it is the cornerstone of the Random Acts of Kindness (RAK) movement, which encourages people to act with kindness towards people in the home, school and community. This has become a worldwide movement with its own foundation (www. randomactsofkindness.org), a RAK week and a series of accompanying lesson plans.

Campaigning

Every major ethical and religious tradition demands action in the face of injustice and inequality. As Mick Waters powerfully argues in Chapter 7, campaigning is closely linked to charitable giving, but, like the famous picture of the young man whose begging bowl sign reads, 'Keep Your Coins I Want Change', one function of education is to develop an understanding of the wider structural causes of inequality and encourage young people to address them.

Courageous

Campaigning requires courage. You have to be brave to stand up for your beliefs and the rights of others. The well-researched and resourced work of Philip Zimbardo's Heroic Imagination Project (HIP) argues that what it calls 'Heroic Imagination' is not only an aspect of compassion but that it can be taught to all young people. HIP seeks to redefine heroism and make it more relevant for a twenty-first-century world. It is no longer the exclusive province of the physically brave, but can be enacted by any individual with firmly held morals and the courage to act on them. Perhaps the most important aspect of heroism is the ability to create positive change in challenging situations (http://heroicimagination.org). Altruism, unlike heroism, Zimbardo argues, involves no personal risk. Acting courageously is a supremely unselfish act that alters how we think. As American scholar and mythologist Joseph Campbell put it: 'When we quit thinking primarily about ourselves and our own self-preservation, we undergo a truly heroic transformation of consciousness' (cited in Mackey-Kallis, 2001: 23).

Emotionally literate

Emotional literacy brings together several of the components of a compassionate person. It forms the basis of the Social and Emotional Aspects of Learning (SEAL) programmes in the UK and the Social and Emotional Learning (SEL) programme in the United States, which encourage self-awareness and regulation, interpersonal and intrapersonal skills, motivation, empathy and compassion.

Empathetic

The English word empathy is derived from the ancient Greek word *empatheia* (physical affection, passion, partiality), which comes from combining *en* (in, at) and *pathos* (passion or suffering). Although empathy can describe a wide range of experiences, it is generally defined as the ability to sense other people's emotions, coupled with the ability to imagine what someone else might be thinking or feeling. Psychologists distinguish between 'affective empathy' and 'cognitive empathy'. Affective empathy refers to the sensations and feelings we get in response to others' emotions. This can include mirroring what that person is feeling (reflective empathy): we learn smiling and laughing, for example, as young children. Affective empathy can show itself when we feel stressed when we detect another's fear or anxiety. Cognitive empathy, sometimes called perspective taking, refers to our ability to identify and understand other people's emotions, our ability to imagine ourselves in their situation. Losing ourselves in storytelling, fantasy and role play are prime examples. Finally, humans also exhibit empathetic joy, the elation we can feel when other people are successful.

Roman Krznaric, in the RSA shorts clip (www.thersa.org/discover/videos/event-videos/2012/02/the-six-habits-of-highly-empathic-people-) and in his wonderful book, *Empathy: A handbook for revolution* (2014), explores these concepts in detail and outlines 'The Six Habits of Highly Empathic People'. For him, the twenty-first century must become an age of 'outrospection', which he contrasts with the twentieth century's age of introspection, where selfishness and consumerism were the dominant drivers. The age of outrospection will be characterized by discovering who we are in relation to other individuals and cultures. For Krznaric, empathy is active and presages radical social change.

Ordinary

Perhaps unsurprisingly, this characteristic provokes the most debate. The sentiment is straightforward: most of us will live relatively ordinary lives, which may never fork lightning, but these lives can be lived in a spirit of kindness and goodness. This was perhaps best summed up by Mother Teresa when she said, 'Not all of us can do great things. But we can do small things with great love.' This is the simple message that young people can understand and act upon.

Reflective

'The unexamined life is not worth living', a famous saying attributed to Socrates, perhaps goes to the heart of a fundamental skill of the compassionate person. Perpetually demanding to know the causes of so many of the world's ills, and of the negative behaviours of others they will encounter, the compassionate person will have a better understanding and may, as a result, act upon their conclusions. Reflection can lead to empathy and empathy to understanding.

Reflexive

That we are not merely neutral observers of the world and that it is impossible to walk in another person's shoes are insights that have widespread acceptance today. Reflexivity is the skill or approach through which we increasingly understand how we ourselves impact on any situation in which we find ourselves.

Sacred

The prophetic words of Black Elk (1863–1950), Sioux shaman and medicine-man, resonate now with the twenty-first-century concern over climate disaster. He urged all humans to 'walk in a sacred manner', to remember Mother Earth with each breath and step. A compassionate person holds and acts upon this advice, for 'sacred' implies something we revere, we hold holy and want to protect; something that, literally, makes us whole. We can see the sacred everywhere and anywhere. For Joseph Campbell, a sacred space is 'a space that is transparent to transcendence and everything within such a space furnishes a base for meditation. This is a place where you can go and feel safe and bring forth what you are and what you might be. This is the place of creative incubation. At first you might find that nothing happens there. But if you have a sacred place and use it, you will eventually find yourself again and again' (cited in the Temple Guy, 2004).

Self-aware

One of the most important skills we can encourage in young people is critical reflection, for this enables them to understand their inner feelings, experiences and behaviours, which in turn helps them to appreciate themselves and others. The development of self-awareness is crucial to their emotional and spiritual development and is an aim shared by humanistic psychology, by all major religious traditions and by many major civilizations. 'Know thyself' is axiomatic to self-realization and to self-actualization. Self-aware people also understand that self-compassion is not the same as narcissistic self-love, but is fundamentally important for their mental and physical health, as they encourage in themselves the behaviours they would wish others to adopt. Mahatma Gandhi captured the sentiment when he exhorted individuals to 'Be the change you wish to see in the world.'

Spiritual

There are heroic echoes of both Zimbardo and Campbell in spirituality as a characteristic of a compassionate person, for spirituality relates to our ultimate sense of meaning and purpose in life; to our relations with our fellows and to that which can be immanent and transcendent.

Sustaining

Sustaining relates both to the individual and to the planet. It is about helping young people to develop inner strength and resilience, so they can withstand the many negative experiences that are part of the human condition. They need to be taught that bad things do happen to good people and that they will make mistakes – sometimes major ones – whatever their intentions. The key is that they reflect upon the causes and then, as far as possible, redress and not repeat the wrongs. It also relates to understanding the wider issues of creating a sustainable planet that meets the needs of all without destroying the environment beyond repair.

Sympathetic

The emotional capacity to be moved by distress but this does not necessarily lead to action.

Visionary

Although the word 'radical' is now over-associated with violent extremism, it is fundamentally important in a world beset with so many major problems that we encourage young people to think 'outside the box', to empathize with the world's problems and attempt to envision solutions for a future based upon compassion. Through adopting this stance, a compassionate person will try to seek equitable solutions.

Many of the above characteristics – like empathy, altruism and kindness – can be seen as overarching principle systems, which are accessible to everybody and have spawned their own educational movements. There are other big ideas that have similar aims to compassionate education but are expressed in different ways. One of the biggest is Character Education, championed by the University of Birmingham's Jubilee Centre for Character and Virtues (www.jubileecentre.ac.uk). Financed by the John Templeton Foundation, it offers a set of key principles and what it calls 'prototypical virtues', which will be recognized by all cultures and religions. Similarly, as part of their local agreed syllabus for religious education, Birmingham City

Council offers resources for developing a set of 24 dispositions, which they describe as 'prevailing qualities of character marked by an inclination, or will to act in a particular way or by a tendency to a certain kind of action' (www.faithmakesadifference.co.uk/dispositions).

In addition, Neil Hawkes, a pioneer of values-based education, has inspired schools and parents globally with his writing (2013), his resources, professional development activities and his website (www.valuesbasededucation.com). Big Picture Learning (www.bigpicture.org), the Human Scale Education movement (www.hse.org.uk) and the YES! for Schools programme (www.youthempowermentseminar.org) all place the development of the individual and relationships at the very heart of curriculum design.

In terms of potential movements, alternative paradigms and ways of working, schools are almost spoilt for choice. Compassion has been central to the major world faiths and is embedded in many faith schools but, to date, very little work has been undertaken on compassionate education in the wider educational context. So why add compassion to a growing list, and why elevate it to *the* organizing principle for schools globally?

Part 2: Why compassion and compassionate education? Why now?

There are ten major drivers that provide the strategic imperatives for compassionate societal and educational change. The majority are positive forces based upon major advances, often in the twenty-first century, in areas like neuroscience, biology and psychology, which confirm much of the wisdom of the ancients and their contemplative practices. Similarly, fundamental changes in the way we learn and communicate, brought about by technological revolution, cause us to challenge the values underpinning our present education systems and provide a dynamic opportunity to galvanize global education on compassionate principles. Politically and socially, these principles have been enshrined in the Charter for Compassion, which is based upon the Golden Rule, 'Treat others as you would wish to be treated' (see Appendix 1). The charter is a mandate for change that sets out to build compassionate thinking into the centre of religious, moral, political, economic and educational life and which, since its inception in 2008, has developed into a dynamic global imperative.

There are negative drivers, however, which are powerful and dangerous and act as siren wake-up calls for the future of the planet. Karen Armstrong, the creative force behind the charter, puts it starkly: 'If we don't manage to implement the Golden Rule globally, so that we treat all peoples, wherever and whoever they may be, as though they were as important as ourselves, I doubt we will have a viable world to hand to the next generation' (Armstrong, 2009). This 'viable' world is being undermined by the ecological consequences of climate change and its political and social repercussions, by growing inequalities of wealth, by an economic system that seems incapable of addressing the needs of our time, and by increasing and often violent intolerance of 'the other'. The negatives have the potential to be resisted but, without compassionate global action, they could outweigh and derail the positives.

The ten self-evident truths: Drivers for compassionate change

i.   That we are all wired for compassion

It seems that our minds shape our brains because the brain's capacity to learn – its neuroplasticity – is altered by our mental activity. Our brains consist of over 100 billion nerve cells (neurons), which are electrically excitable and which process and transmit information through electrical and chemical signals. These signals travel via synapses, the tiny gaps across which one neuron can send an impulse to another. When all your neurons 'fire' together, they strengthen existing ones, create new ones and 'wire' them together. This wiring together allows learning and new insights.

It follows, therefore, that the life experiences we enjoy (and suffer) can alter the brain's activity and its structure, which in turn reinforce the brain's wiring. Acting compassionately stimulates the brain chemical, dopamine, which encourages us to feel good, so we are more likely to repeat these actions, forming a virtuous circle. The opposite equally applies. Acting badly can lead to the production of the stress-related chemical, cortisone, which in turn alters our neural pathways.

The brain is deeply social and we know that how, and to whom we communicate alters its circuitry and our actions. The key is the experiences we have and the motivations that follow. As Dan Siegel writes in the Foreword to *Buddha's Brain* (Hanson, 2009: v), 'the simple truth is that how we focus our attention, how we intentionally direct the flow of energy and information through our neural circuits, can directly alter the brain's activity and its structure'. As Hanson puts it, 'What flows through your mind sculpts your brain. Thus *you can use your mind to change your brain for the better* – which will benefit your whole being, and every other person whose life you touch' (6).

In recent years, there has been a deluge of evidence in the fields of psychophysiology, biology, neuroscience and psychology, demonstrating that human beings are instinctually compassionate – a trait that appears genetically programmed. In addition, science verifies that the purposeful cultivation of compassion allows us to galvanize the social circuits of the brain, which can transform relationships with others and even with our own self. The inescapable conclusion, maintains James R. Doty, Founder and Director of the Center for Compassion and Altruism Research and Education (CCARE) at Stanford, is that 'our brains are wired for compassion' (http://ccare.stanford.edu).

Advances in psychological understanding support those made in neuroscience and psychophysiology. In particular, the innovative work of psychologist and compassion-focused therapist Professor Paul Gilbert has enhanced our understanding of what he terms the 'compassionate mind'. Through his research, his writings and the Compassionate Mind Foundation (www.compassionatemind.co.uk), we gain insights into the opposing natures of 'old brain psychologies' that humans developed thousands of years ago to help survive in dangerous times, and which can still predispose us towards negativity. The 'old brain' conflicts with 'new brain' competences and abilities including traits like imagination, reflection and purposeful focusing of the mind. Crucial for schools, this purposeful focusing can be taught through meditative techniques known as mindfulness. Mindfulness is a non-judgemental, moment-by-moment awareness of thoughts, feelings, bodily sensations and surrounding environment. Though its roots are in Buddhist meditative practices, it is an international secular movement that teaches practitioners that you are not your thoughts, not your emotions.

For Gilbert, Hanson, Doty and other scientists, compassion can be cultivated and maintained through purposeful mindfulness training, just like improving your physical fitness. This brings enormous benefits to the individual but also, as Jonathan Haidt at the University of Virginia has shown, compassionate actions can inspire others who in their turn become more likely to act compassionately, thus completing the virtuous circle. Education, however, with the possible exception of areas like child and adolescent mental health, and special educational needs, has come late to the scientific party.

There are growth areas, however. Mindfulness training in schools appears to have caught on and organizations like the Greater Good Science Center at the University of California, Berkeley offer the latest scientific insights, many of them education focused. Science demonstrates that our innate capacity for compassion can be enhanced by teaching compassion, and by teaching and learning in a compassionate manner. Proven links between that and increases in cognitive abilities are largely inferred, but work such as Annie Murphy-Paul's *Brilliant: The new science of smart* (2015) is addressing the issue.

ii.   That the Golden Rule, treat others (and the Earth) as you would wish to be treated, is central to the world's ethical and religious traditions

Since its inception in 2008, the Charter for Compassion has had an immense impact. A visit to its website (http://charterforcompassion.org) reveals its growing influence in all walks of life. More and more cities across the globe are joining the network of compassionate communities, and they are encouraged and supported by a growing resource body. Communities sign up to the charter and agree to devise and implement an action plan to make the Golden Rule a reality. In addition, there is a dedicated schools charter for compassion where schools can make a public commitment to act compassionately (http://charterforcompassion.org/education-book). Implicit within the rule is care for the planet, which is invariably found within the body of the religious and secular texts but now, in the light of the climate change crisis, needs to be made explicit. That is why we argue for a 21st-century version 'treat others (and the Earth) as you would wish to be treated'.

The charter is one of the major drivers for compassion but there are others. Annually since 2012, the Tenzin Gyatso Institute, together with Stanford CCARE, has run major conferences for professionals, accompanied by a youth gathering. These 'Empathy and Compassion in Society' gatherings have provided a universal overview of compassionate developments in research and in practice. Many of the key speeches are available online (http://compassioninsociety.org) and provide an inspirational resource in the dynamically expanding field.

Faith and interfaith groups provide added impetus. Their part in building cohesion is usefully explored in a UK toolkit available from what was called the Centre for Social Cohesion at the University of Coventry (Coles, 2007). The Golden Rule is central to all Abrahamic faiths and each, in its own way, translates this into practice in the social sphere. For many, 'engaged Buddhism' acts as a major draw as it is non-theistic and encourages loving-kindness (*metta*) as a key virtue (Thera, 2013).

The implementation of the Golden Rule is common to all compassionate organizations but so is the Golden Thread, although it may not be articulated in the same way. Like the rule, the Golden Thread is time honoured and is the active component of 'love in action', which permeates adherents' lives and, as the metaphor suggests, is woven into their daily interactions. One of its manifestations is the principle of service, of doing good works, often without reward. Service is central to humanistic and faith-based traditions. Each faith has its own unique vocabulary. The word 'service' has Christian roots. In Islam, it is known as *khidma*, in Hinduism as Karma Yoga, and in Sikhism as *sewa* or selfless service. In Judaism, individuals perform *mitzvot*, good deeds, which are also central to all Buddhist schools. For all these religions, serving humanity is serving God/Ultimate Being and the highest and noblest manifestation is for humans to act as true guardians and stewards of the planet.

iii.   That compassion is essential for good mental and physical health

We understand both the causes and the consequences of the epidemic of ill-health that characterizes the Western world and increasingly the developing world. The Global Health Observatory (www.who.int/gho/en) produces alarming statistics on the number of suicides, mental health issues, violence against women and children, and incidences of malnutrition. Most nation states compile their own detailed statistics which, when added to figures related to our ageing populations, provide a frightening backdrop to our paradigm shift.

iv.   That successful organizations are built on compassionate values

Values based upon happiness and contentment form the heart of many successful companies. Over 30 years ago, Peters and Waterman in their seminal *In Search of Excellence* (1982), stressed the importance of values in the corporate business world. As they put it, 'Every excellent company we studied is clear on what it stands for, and takes the process of value shaping seriously. In fact, we wonder whether it is possible to be an excellent company without clarity on values and without having the right sort of values' (280). More recently, based upon years of empirical research and practical implementation, Richard Barrett, founder of Barrett Values Centre, has helped to transform numerous companies into successful values-driven organizations.

Barrett champions a new leadership paradigm, which begins with the individual (leading self) and, by degrees, expands through leading organizations to leading in society. Corporate organizations are now the most powerful on the planet, and innovative thinkers like Barrett and Frederic Laloux offer clearly thought-out structural and leadership models to help organizations become inspired by what Laloux (2014: 6) calls 'the next stage of human consciousness'. Both their paradigms are based upon a clear sense of moral purpose, the *explicit* intention to make a positive difference in the lives of employees, customers and society as a whole; and, perhaps more surprisingly, an emphasis on the spiritual, on the soul of employees and organizations.

Similarly, movements like Conscious Capitalism, which strive for a greater sense of moral purpose in business (www.consciouscapitalism. org/purpose), are gaining serious ground. Many companies now subscribe to a 'Triple Bottom Line' model of success, wherein they aim to provide positive value in the '3Ps' – people, planet and profit. Bronwyn Fryer, in her article 'The rise of compassionate management (finally)' (2013), explores these concepts and the practices in more detail. Fryer cites Wisdom 2.0, an organization dedicated to 'exploring living with greater awareness, wisdom and compassion in the modern age'. She quotes LinkedIn's CEO, Jeff Weiner, who told a Wisdom 2.0 conference that he is on a personal mission to 'expand the world's collective wisdom and compassion', and that he had made the practice of compassionate management a core value at the company. Managing compassionately, Weiner argued, doesn't come naturally to most managers. It requires spending the time to walk in someone else's shoes: understanding what kind of baggage that person is bringing to work; what kinds of stresses they are under; what their strengths and weaknesses are.

v.   That technology has the power to become a vehicle for compassion

Technology, with a degree of immediacy unknown hitherto, provides us with a wonderful vehicle to walk in someone else's shoes. Probably the greatest power of the age, the Internet, has the capacity to connect us globally anytime and anywhere. It is amazing that such a recent invention has, it is estimated, been accessed by more than a third of the world's population. It also has enormous power to spread discord and violence but as Wisdom 2.0 contends, the great challenge is not merely to live, connected to one another through technology, but to do so in ways that are beneficial to our own well-being, effective in our work and useful to the world. We are all globally interconnected with an inconceivable immediacy and, as many of us have observed, young people can access and utilize these digital technologies and the social media with ease.

These technologies have the power to transform how we learn and to help us to become more compassionate and empathetic human beings, though this potential has yet to be effectively realized. The collaborative processes underpinning Sugata Mitra's pioneering 'Hole in the Wall' experiments, which have morphed into the ultimate 'School in the Cloud' (Mitra, 2013), offer one possible road map. Mitra and his teams have proved that groups of children, whatever their social and educational backgrounds, can, with access to the Internet, learn almost anything by themselves. Mitra's Self Organized Learning Environments (SOLEs) and online mentoring scheme, Self-Organized Mediation Environment (SOME), provide the ideal tools to make compassionate journeys. The essential beauty of a SOLE is that, without direct teacher intervention, it encourages young people to collaborate, ask and then discover the answers to the big questions the planet faces.

vi.   That many of the world's cities are places of hyper-diversity

England, like other countries, is now a place of super/hyper-diversity with a population that includes a vast range of cultures, heritages, languages, faiths and ethnicities. Cities have become microcosms of the world's populations. The implications for our education services are profound as teachers have to provide a curriculum, pedagogy and set of values that help all children to both achieve and live together harmoniously in these multicultural global societies.

vii.   That man-made climate change, and the evils of terror and counter-terror, have the potential to undermine the forces of compassion

'Science has spoken. There is no ambiguity in the message.' The ringing words of the UN Secretary-General, Ban Ki-moon, at the launch of the 'historic' report of the UN Intergovernmental Panel on Climate Change (IPCC), were clear. Climate change is 'set to inflict severe, widespread and irreversible impacts' on people and the natural world unless carbon emissions are cut sharply and rapidly (IPCC, 2014). This report, in a long line of similar reports, paints a frightening vision of the legacy we will leave our children and grandchildren. There is no doubt as to who is to blame. The 2,009-page IPCC report judged that it was 'unequivocal' that climate change was the result of human actions and warned that, without 'substantial and sustained' reductions in greenhouse gas emissions, we will breach the symbolic threshold of 2°C of warming, with consequences so calamitous that their effects could last for hundreds if not thousands of years. Many of the effects are already apparent: severe weather, drought, flood, famine and now predictions that our actions are leading to the Earth facing the sixth great (and first man-made) species extinction (www.biologicaldiversity.org).

This message is hardly new. Former US Vice President, Al Gore, in his 2006 film, *An Inconvenient Truth – A Global Warning*, explains the causes of climate change and the genesis, trajectory and frighteningly dystopic view of the scientists who sought to counter it. For Gore, and his new ally, Pharrell Williams (see Hann, 2015), it is primarily a moral issue, one that the world's leaders are failing to act upon, although we have the technology to make those changes. The IPCC report, like Gore's film, suggests a number of solutions that it is argued are both affordable and actionable.

Some argue that this is a spiritual as well as a moral and economic issue. *Spiritual Ecology: The cry of the Earth*, edited by Llewellyn Vaughan-Lee (2013b), provides a series of essays from a range of traditions, which describe the intimate and symbiotic connection between human beings and the sacred nature of creation. The contribution of the late Thomas Berry, Catholic priest and eco-theologian, captures its essence when he wrote: 'There is now a single issue before us: survival. Not merely physical survival, but survival in a world of fulfilment, survival in a living world, where the violets bloom in the spring time, where the stars shine down in all their mystery, survival in world of meaning' (Vaughan-Lee, 2013b: 17).

Amazingly, it was as late as 2013 that the United States agreed non-binding guidelines on the teaching of climate change, and even those were considerably watered down from the earlier drafts (Goldenberg, 2013). Frighteningly, the inexplicable removal of climate change from the 2014 English primary school National Curriculum (DfE, 2013a) and any reference to sustainable development from the secondary one (DfE, 2014a), reinforces many of the points made over 20 years ago in David Orr's *Earth in Mind*, when he argued that 'without significant precautions, education can equip people merely to be more effective vandals of the earth' (Orr, 1994: 6).

'Effective vandals of the earth' could easily form the subtext to any examination of terrorism and responses to it. At present, we are locked into a vicious cycle of terror – whether it is faith- or state-inspired – and reactive counter-terror, which can be, for example, anti-Islamic, anti-imperialistic, or antisemitic. The causes of terror are many, complex and hotly disputed. It is impossible to divorce them from the wider geopolitical issues that relate to our consumption of oil and gas, and foreign policies based upon defending the West's strategic influence in the Middle East. They do not lend themselves, however, to a simplistic Manichean view of the universe, of good versus evil. Nor do they lend themselves to simple crude solutions where the good guys beat the bad guys. The consequences, however, are clear, in terms of innocent human lives lost and a circle of hate.

viii. That our present economic system does not encourage compassion

'Effective vandals of the earth' could likewise form the subtext to discussion about our present economic system which, to adapt an IPCC (2014) phrase about delays in combating climate change, is 'dangerous and profoundly irrational'. Empirical research increasingly demonstrates that the global neoliberal economic system is not working. Or, perhaps more accurately, it works for a tiny minority, in terms of increasing wealth and income accumulation at the expense of the massive majority. The predominant economic orthodoxy, articulated with passionate simplicity by Boris Johnson, Mayor of London (see Stanley, 2013), argues that being super-rich and highly paid in free market economies is a good and necessary thing because it generates wealth that 'trickles down' to the poor, thereby enriching all. The reality is, however, starkly different. Britain and the United States are now two of the most unequal and divided places on earth. In the UK, five families own more than the poorest 20% combined (Oxfam, 2014) and levels of societal inequality have surpassed those of Edwardian England. The situation is even worse in the United States. As Eric Zeusse put it in the *Huffington Post* (2013), 'according to the world's most thorough study of wealth distribution the United States has such an unequal distribution of wealth ... that it's in the league of corrupt underdeveloped countries, no longer in the league of the developed nations.'

Not only does this fire our sense of moral outrage because of its unfairness, but it is bad economics. As the International Monetary Fund (IMF, 2015) has pointed out, ever greater concentrations of wealth and income actually hinder growth. Redistribution would not just reduce inequality but would be economically beneficial. This argument is central to Thomas Piketty's massively researched *Capital in the Twenty-First Century* (2014). He argues that wealth that is unrelated to production produces more wealth and those who aspire to join the super-rich play a constant game of catch-up and demand a larger and larger slice of income generated, normally at the expense of the lower paid. It is not merely a matter of untrammelled individual greed, but a product of the system working normally.

In *The Spirit Level: Why equality is better for everyone* (2010), Wilkinson and Pickett offer a detailed and searing analysis of the outcomes of large-scale inequalities. They demonstrate that almost everything, from life expectancy to mental illness, from levels of violence to levels of illiteracy, is affected not by how wealthy a society is but by how equal it is. We have been sold an impossible consumerists' dream of ever-rising living standards in a system that simply cannot deliver.

The sad truth appears to be that consumerism, competition and individual acquisition of wealth, upon which the present system rests, do not deliver and do not lead to happiness and contentment. In his article in the *Guardian*, 'Materialism: a system that eats us from the inside out', George Monbiot (2013) parades the evidence that reveals that not only is there a strong correlation between materialism and a lack of empathy and engagement, as well as depression and loneliness, but that the more materialistic people become, the unhappier they get. The obverse appears equally true: being compassionate and generous makes you a better and happier person. As Tom Williams, Co-Chair of the Partnership for a Compassionate Louisville, Kentucky – the 'world's most compassionate city'– put it in a speech at Compassion Week (November 2014), 'Compassion is not like money, which if you give it away it diminishes. With compassion, if you give it away it increases.'

Our politicians concentrate on economic growth but, as the economist Richard Layard, one of the founders of Action for Happiness (www.actionforhappiness.org), argues in *Happiness: Lessons from a new science* (2011) and in *A Good Childhood: Searching for values in a competitive age* (2009), what is required is a new paradigm with happiness and contentment as key measures of our children's and our nation's well-being.

ix.   That compassion can be caught, taught, and cultivated

These three concepts are unpacked in detail in Part 3 below.

x.   That compassion can become education's key unifying meta-value; its central organizing principle

Sympathy, altruism, kindness and empathy can all be seen as essential building blocks of compassion, in that compassion incorporates their attributes into the identification of, feeling with and responding to suffering. Simply expressed as 'love in action', compassion can act as the unifying meta-value that people of all ages can easily make an everyday lived experience. It is probably the simplest, oldest and most intuitive concept in human history.

Part 3: So what is compassionate education? The five Cs of compassion

We have a new context. The ten drivers provide the imperatives and the urgency for change. 'Acts for love' offer a taxonomy of values. Neuroscience proves that we are wired for compassion; and now we need a new story, a new paradigm upon which to operate, one in which **collaboration and service** replace competition and consumerism. Education is at the foothills of these changes and each of our following chapters offers more detailed analyses of aspects of the compassionate school. In summary, however, **compassionate education is the conscious implementation of love in action, of the values and virtues outlined in the mnemonic 'acts for love'. It involves making compassion the organizing principle of everything we do. It embraces the** spiritual, moral, social, cultural and intellectual development of students and of society, as well as their physical and mental health. It includes faith and interfaith approaches as well as secular movements devoted to values and character education, to educating the heart, to emotional literacy and to the building of empathy and resilience. Compassion in education is both product-based – curriculum, organization, systems – and process-driven – meditation, mindfulness, dialogic reasoning, empathetic listening, the power of the narrative and co-creation. It is predicated upon five building blocks, the five Cs of compassion.

The first C, **compassionate consciousness**, is a perspective that should permeate every aspect of school life. To translate this into action, however, schools need to create **a culture of compassion**, the second C, which in turn helps to produce the third C, **a compassionate climate**. The **compassionate curriculum**, the fourth C, involves every aspect of school life, including the taught and hidden curricula. All of which must culminate in the final C, **compassionate action** – for staff, for pupils and for parents and communities.

Becoming a compassionate school: Caught, taught, and cultivated

How is this to be achieved? Each school will develop its own unique path depending on its present position. The school will use its existing cyclical school improvement processes to achieve its aims. Many schools will recognize that much of what they are already doing qualifies, and what is required is a shift in emphasis, a restatement of values, a reorienting of practice. To become genuinely compassionate, all stakeholders, including pupils, should be involved in the process in age-appropriate ways. This book is called *Towards the Compassionate School* because education is always a journey to goals that shift according to context and time, but which should have, at their foundation, a set of fundamental and timeless compassionate principles. Compassion can be directly taught – you can learn about compassion, about how the brain works, about the actions of great compassionate teachers like Mother Teresa, Mahatma Gandhi and Martin Luther King, all of whom spoke and wrote about and lived compassion. It can also be taught via meditation and mindfulness.

Surprisingly, however, for such a time-honoured concept there is little systematic guidance to support schools on their compassionate journey. Paul D. Houston, in his Foreword to Johnson and Neagley's *Educating From the Heart* (2011), refers to 'the vast void in current practice', which the book attempts to fill. It not only offers a useful range of perspectives on varied meanings of 'educating with heart and spirit' (Johnson and Neagley, 2011: xxiii), but also provides a variety of practical approaches. These include contributions from nine practising teachers who describe their various classroom and curriculum approaches, which range from 'teaching children empathy' to 'counselling from the heart', and a detailed programme entitled 'integrating the spirit with total body fitness' (see Wood and Higgins, 2011: 111).

Marshall Rosenberg, founder of the seminally influential concept of non-violent communication (NVC), has for many years offered compassion-based training. In 2004, his work inspired *The Compassionate Classroom: Relationship-based teaching and learning* by Sura Hart and Victoria Kindle Hodson, one of the first books to outline the principles and practices of a compassionate elementary/primary school. Similarly, Pamela Cayton, designer of the Creating Compassionate Cultures programme and Headteacher of the Tara Redwood School in California, systematically outlines the aims and principles of a compassionate school, provides seven steps to achieve it, offers a range of methodologies for adoption and a number of sample lesson plans in her excellent book, *Compassion in Education: An introduction to creating compassionate cultures* (2011). It is the fruit of over 25 years of headship at the school and is backed up by a supportive online training course (www.creatingcompassionatecultures.com). Her 'Guidelines for Teachers' (2011: 14) suggest a number of key characteristics of the compassionate teacher, including: the teacher as firm but loving guide; the teacher who hears the children's point of view; and the teacher who can 'enjoy life as it comes: be serious about humour and plan for spontaneity'. Pam Cayton's work is linked to that of the London-based Foundation for Developing Compassion and Wisdom (www.compassionandwisdom.org), which offers an international range of courses and resources designed to foster peace, harmony, mindfulness and emotional resilience. The Foundation's *16 Guidelines for a Happy Life*, written by Alison Murdoch and Dekyi-Lee Oldershaw (2009), outlines the principles of 'universal education'. Based upon the work of the seventh-century Buddhist King Songsten Gampo of Tibet, the guidelines are underpinned by four philosophic themes: How We Think, How We Act, How We Relate and How We Find Meaning. Teachers across the globe have found the Foundation's essentially practical and incremental work to be of great value.

Equally practical and valuable is the work of the Mary Gordon. Her Roots of Empathy Foundation (www.rootsofempathy.org) and accompanying book, *Roots of Empathy: Changing the world child by child* (2009), offer a customized emotional literacy programme wherein, over the course of a year, students enjoy and reflect upon the progress and behaviour of an infant who visits the school with their parents every three weeks. The programme is specifically designed for pupils from kindergarten/nursery age to 9 years.

Geared to older students is *The Compassionate Classroom: Lessons that nurture wisdom and empathy* (Dalton and Fairchild, 2004). The authors outline 40 lessons clustered in the four seasons. Each lesson is prefaced by a key question: for example, 'How do I establish the moral foundation of my classroom?' (6). They expand on their theme and provide a number of lesson ideas. Each one ends with a teacher reflection, such as, 'When do I find myself smiling in my classroom?' (116).

Compassion can also be 'caught', learned by young people as they, without conscious thought, model their behaviours on those they look up to. How teachers and parents behave, and how pupils behave to each other, is fundamental to the transmission of compassionate values. A compassionately cultured school reinforces positive messages. Compassion can be cultivated purposefully and systematically through the curriculum we adopt, the content we choose, the pedagogies we employ, the evaluations we undertake. The chapters in the present book are peppered with practical examples of cultivation, whether it be mindfulness training, social and moral aspects of education, or curriculum drivers. Appendix 2 provides a short list of initiatives already underway, many of which have their own supportive lesson plans. This list is taken from the CoED Foundation's NICEN (National and International Compassion in Education Network) web page, which aims to create a dynamic informal electronic network of compassionate education organizations to which educators can hyperlink. In addition, NICEN contains examples of good practice, and short subject-based think pieces, like Talal Hussain's 'The Compassionate Mathematician'.

Thus, we understand the nature of compassion, its component parts. We recognize it intuitively as love in action, and cognitively as 'acts for love'. The imperatives for change are clear and overwhelming, and slowly the pathways are being mapped and trodden. The end is clear. We must produce a global compassionate education service, must change the story so that future generations inherit a world based on love, with collaboration and service at its core.

Chapter 2

Compassionate minds (and brains) in education

Tamara A. Russell and Tiago P. Tatton-Ramos

Abstract

Neuroscience data related to the developing brain and 'brain-informed' ways of working in the classroom is attracting increasing attention. The field of contemplative neuroscience is fast expanding and bringing into the mainstream neuroanatomical terminology and findings from neuroimaging studies to help us to understand what happens in the brain when we learn to pay attention, moment by moment, without judgement, and the benefits this brings to the educational setting. These studies are challenging the assumption that the brain follows a single predetermined developmental trajectory. Rather, we are learning that the brain is highly plastic and much more malleable than previously thought.

This chapter begins with a brief review of the current literature as it relates to mindfulness and compassionate mind training. Although the majority of these studies have been conducted with adults, many of the findings have direct implications for how we work with our young people in the classroom to help them build healthier neural networks that will equip them with the skills they need to function as emotionally resilient and resourceful adults. We consider the training requirements for teachers to deliver mindfulness in the classroom and also describe the changes observed in the brain following these distinct but related trainings. This clinical, educational and imaging data indicates that mindfulness of the body is the key to engaging with our own emotional experiences in a more skilful and compassionate way and that this, in turn, is a vital building block in developing the ability to be more compassionate towards others.

Mindfulness and compassion training in the secular context

A growing body of research indicates that mindfulness training confers a variety of positive benefits, ranging from improvements in self-reported quality of life to changes in the immune system, brain connectivity and genetic expression (Carlson *et al.*, 2007; Chiesa and Serretti, 2009; Creswell *et al.*, 2012; Davidson *et al.*, 2003; Eberth and Sedlmeier, 2012; Williams and Penman, 2012). These interventions draw on Buddhist psychological models of the mind but have been secularized for use in modern-day healthcare (and wider) systems. Mindfulness is defined by Kabat-Zinn (1982) as a type of awareness that arises from paying attention to our experiences (internal and external), purposefully, moment by moment and without judgement. This latter aspect, 'without judgement', requires us to practise being kind to ourselves no matter what we are experiencing and, from this, we learn to be kind and more accepting of others. We start with kindness on the inside, to our own thoughts and feelings, and this ripples outwards into our relationships and wider life.

Current mindfulness trainings range between five and ten weeks, with one meeting of approximately two to three hours each week, and are usually in a group. A number of meta-analyses and systematic reviews of mindfulness-based interventions (MBIs) indicate that mental and physical health benefits are attainable – even for those with longstanding chronic and disabling mental and physical health conditions (Carlson *et al.*, 2007; Carlson, 2012; Cusens *et al.*, 2010; Grossman *et al.*, 2004; Jacobsen *et al.*, 2011). As the benefits of mindfulness are demonstrated with adults and across increasingly diverse settings, there is a growing interest in their application for younger people and in education (Kuyken *et al.*, 2013). Here, the focus of the work is the development of skills that build emotional resilience and help to prevent the emergence of common mental health conditions (e.g. depression and anxiety). Data from the Mental Health Foundation (www.mentalhealth.org.uk) suggests that one in four people in the UK will experience a mental health problem each year, while one in six experience a neurotic disorder such as anxiety or depression. Anxiety disorders are also estimated to affect 3.3% of children and young adults in the UK. For this reason, in the UK, education has become a main target for the delivery of mindfulness and this topic is under consideration by a governmental Mindfulness All Party Parliamentary Group (http://oxfordmindfulness.org/all-party-parliamentary-launch).

As the mindfulness research field develops, there remain questions about the operationalization and measurement of the concept, the durability of the effects, the main ingredients driving the effects and the requirements for training secular mindfulness teachers (Brewer *et al.*,

2011; Carmody and Baer, 2008; Holzel *et al.*, 2011; Schonert-Reichl and Lawlor, 2010). This latter point has direct relevance to the teaching of mindfulness and compassion in the school setting. The mindfulness experience of the teacher/facilitator certainly seems to have a direct bearing on the clinical outcomes found in studies with adults (Khoury *et al.*, 2013).

One important finding in the adult literature is that changes in the various outcome measures are often linked to changes in self-compassion. This was reported in an early study by Shapiro *et al.* (2007), in a group of healthcare workers who completed an eight-week mindfulness-based stress reduction (MBSR) training. Changes in scores on the Perceived Stress Scale were correlated with changes in self-compassion (Cohen-Katz *et al.*, 2004). As self-compassion increased, staff reported less perceived stress. The word 'perceived' is important here because mindfulness training does not promise to give us a life free from stress; rather, it is an invitation to learn more skilful ways of dealing with the challenges we face. This work suggests that a large part of the stress we experience is related to our own internal critical voice and that when we can work more kindly with this, our perceived stress goes down.

In the UK, the eight-week mindfulness-based cognitive therapy (MBCT) training is offered as a treatment for chronic major depression and is in the National Institute for Health and Care Excellence (NICE) guidance as a recommended treatment for those with three or more episodes of depression. A number of large-scale trials have been conducted and it has been shown that changes in self-compassion mediate the improvements in mental health following this training (Kuyken *et al.*, 2010). People learn to be kinder to themselves when they notice they are slipping into negative ruminative thinking patterns or self-judgement. This change in attitude begins to permeate all thinking, actions and interactions. Each time a thought is met with curiosity and acceptance (rather than resistance, fear or anger), this is a mini droplet of kindness and compassion. This process is repeated over and over again in formal practices (for example, putting aside time to do a practice such as the bodyscan: www.mindful.org/mindfulness-practice/the-body-scan-practice), as well as during informal practices (e.g. noticing when we are doing something that is not kind and taking an alternate action). What happens in the mind generalizes out into our actions in the world, prompting more compassionate acts towards ourselves and others.

Changes in self-compassion have been shown in one study to be a better predictor than changes in mindfulness for the reduction of symptoms of anxiety and depression and improvements in quality of life (Van Dam *et al.*, 2011). Woodruff *et al.* (2013) showed that self-compassion and psychological inflexibility may demonstrate greater associations with psychological health than single scores of mindfulness. This work suggests that, although mindfulness is important, it needs to be considered alongside training in compassion and that the compassion aspect may be even more important for our mental health. The research is telling us that the general abilities of self-regulation and psychological flexibility promoted by mindfulness training are not simply boosted by the compassion training components, but actually depend upon them (Jazaieri *et al.*, 2014). Thus, there is good evidence that a key element of mindfulness training is the change in self-compassion that is first deliberately practised and then, eventually, embodied.

Mindfulness, compassion and schools environments

Given the challenges of the modern classroom, the alarming increase in mental health difficulties in our young people (Burke, 2010) and the stress placed on teachers (Lavian, 2012; Zabel and Zabel, 2001), it is vital that some form of training to support and encourage emotional resilience and competency is considered. Many authors from the field of Social and Emotional Learning have described the importance of training in these so-called 'soft skills' (Schonert-Reichl and Lawlor, 2010) in order for our children to thrive in what is likely to be an uncertain work (and world) environment.

Internationally, there is an effort to engage in this process, and mindfulness and compassion training in the classroom seems to be one approach gaining ground. This work is also being conducted in child and adolescent mental health settings (in the same way that it initially developed in the adult mental and physical health arena), but there is increasing interest in using this training to prevent mental health difficulties from developing, rather than as a treatment (Huppert and Johnson, 2010). It is clear that adaptations of the adult programmes are required to make them suitable for young people and for delivery in the classroom setting (Thompson and Gauntlett-Gilbert, 2008). Some of these are listed in Figure 2.1.

☐ Shorter duration of practices
☐ Less emphasis on homework
☐ Engagement of parents or carers
☐ More informal practices (finding moments to be mindful rather than deliberately sitting in a practice)
☐ Increasing the variety of practices (including use of technology such as phones)
☐ Use of metaphors
☐ Use of the five senses

Figure 2.1: Adaptations required for teaching mindfulness to children

Zinger (2011) developed the following list to describe an ideal scenario that a mindful and compassionate classroom could create:

- Imagine a classroom ...
  - where there is minimal waste of time, confusion or disruption
  - where a no-nonsense, work-oriented tone prevails but there is a relaxed pleasant atmosphere
  - where mutual respect is established
  - where non-judgemental views are expressed when tackling controversial topics
  - where we develop realistic ways of teaching and learning that move us toward compassion and tolerance.

A recent special issue of the journal *Research in Human Development* was published exploring the benefits of MBI in schools (Frank, Jennings, and Greenberg, 2013: 1). In the introduction, the editors stated that 'mindfulness can be used to help to improve student–teacher relationships, reduce ADHD symptomology, promote emotion regulation, and reduce stress among school-age youth'.

A study from Murphy *et al.* (2012) found that college students (median age of 19 years old) with greater mindfulness skills tend to have better quality of sleep, diet and physical health. A ten-week MBI conducted in Australia found that youngsters between the ages of 10 and 12 reduced symptoms of depression and developed better coping mechanisms after participating in an MBI (Joyce *et al.*, 2010).

There seems to be a similar effectiveness for mindfulness training in young people as demonstrated in adults in the health field (Huppert and Johnson, 2010; Rotne and Rotne, 2013). This means that both teachers and students who undergo training in mindfulness are able to improve on general indicators of well-being, care and compassion, while reducing stress and other physical and psychological difficulties (Bei *et al.*, 2013; Kuyken *et al.*, 2013; White, 2012). Below, we briefly describe the approaches where empirical data has been collected on the training protocols. There are a number of other protocols under development and in use and much variation and idiosyncrasy in approach. Note that, although the focus is often on the mindfulness training, the compassion element is contained within that, even when not explicitly taught.

Shapiro's model

Shapiro's model of the mechanism of mindfulness helps to illuminate this point. Her model includes three 'axioms' (Shapiro *et al.*, 2006) – attention, intention and attitude, as shown in Figure 2.2. This diagram makes it clear that we might move between these three axioms as we are practising: trying our best to pay attention, deliberately intending to complete the practice and, in any and every way possible, adopting an attitude of acceptance, curiosity and kindness. Each time we intend to attend to our mental and physical experience, it is essential to engage in this process with a particular attitude conveying a quality of compassion and acceptance. It is possible to have an attentional training where the stance is hard, cold and scrutinizing. This would be against the central tenets of the mindfulness practice, which encourages the acceptance of all phenomena of the mind, be they 'pleasant' or 'unpleasant', wanted or not wanted. This is the 'radical acceptance' Tara Brach speaks of: the ability to welcome and embrace even the darkest thoughts and most shameful images (Brach, 2004). Only from this practice is liberation from our own mentally created suffering possible. Within Bishop *et al.* (2004), operational definition of mindfulness is the notion of an *accepting* orientation to experience. From these models, we can clearly see that mindfulness and compassion are interwoven.

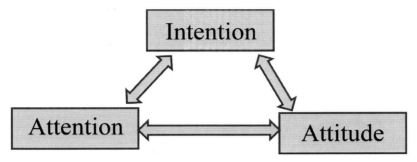

Figure 2.2: Adaptation of Shapiro's model of mindfulness
Source: Shapiro *et al.* (2006)

Goetz *et al.*, (2010) also define compassion as 'the emotion one experiences when feeling concern for another's suffering and desiring to enhance that individual's welfare'. Compassion is composed, therefore, of two aspects: firstly, the affective or emotional component; secondly, the call to action, a pro-social motivational component. Klimecki *et al.* (2013) distinguish this from empathy, which is the affective component alone, as we feel someone's pain alongside them.

.b (dot-be)

The Mindfulness in Schools Project (MiSP) or .b (dot-be) is a curriculum-based intervention developed over four years, with the input of more than 200 teachers who have been trained to incorporate a mindful and compassionate way of teaching (http://mindfulnessinschools.org). The basis of the .b protocol includes adaptations of mindfulness training techniques deriving from standardized protocols, including MBSR and MBCT. It is directly linked to the adult evidence base. During the .b training, across nine weekly meetings, teachers and students are encouraged to include mindfulness and compassion in their personal and professional lives through a series of conceptual didactic and experiential explorations. The programme was created to meet the needs of school-age children but, because of the promising results, has been expanded to preschool (paws .b) and even adults.

In the MiSP, each one of the nine sessions aims to teach a distinct mindfulness skill through a way to motivate the engagement of young minds. The lessons include a brief presentation by the teacher with the help of lively, pupil-friendly visuals, film and sound images, and practical exercises and demonstrations to make the ideas vivid and relevant to pupils' lives. The people who developed the programme for young people claim that it is not 'adult mindfulness' because the 'course is shorter and the messages punchier and more direct and the practices and discussions briefer. The goals are more modest, and include simply making all pupils aware of the existence of mindfulness in case they wish to explore it later.'

Research on the accessibility and impact of the .b programme in schools has been conducted with those in the age range 12–16, as this is a 'key developmental window for self-regulation and a period when young people need to negotiate many academic and social stressors for the first time'. The results indicated that this training was acceptable to both students and teachers and provides a promising way to improve young people's skills to work with mental states, everyday life and stressors so as to cultivate well-being and promote mental health (Kuyken *et al.*, 2013). In May 2014, a number of young people who had undergone .b training at school reported on their experience to the UK's Mindfulness All Party Parliamentary Group. Their ability to speak in front of an audience of parliamentarians and lords was already impressive but their descriptions of how they were using mindfulness in their daily life, to help with academic, athletic, interpersonal and family challenges, bringing awareness and kindness into their lives, conveyed the real power of this approach.

MindUP

MindUP (http://thehawnfoundation.org/mindup) is one of the growing number of mindful educational (ME) programmes spearheaded by The Hawn Foundation. It is a research-based training protocol for educators and children of various ages, currently available via Scholastic publishers. These mindful practices, embedded into classroom learning, are seen as central to the programme with the intention of enhancing children's self-awareness, focused attention, self-regulation and stress reduction. To foster optimism and positive affect, affirmations and visualizations are practised in conjunction with mindful practices (Schonert-Reichl and Lawlor, 2010).

The key components of the MindUP programme include:

1) quieting the mind (by paying attention to a resonating instrument (chime), while focusing on breath)

2) mindful attention (to a variety of sensations, thoughts and feelings)

3) managing negative emotions and negative thinking

4) acknowledgement of self and others.

Over ten weeks, the children undergo a ten-lesson curriculum, based on a standardized manual, with clear lesson plans grounded in theory and research, and an emphasis on taking lesson content and extending its components to other aspects of the curriculum and other dimensions of children's lives outside school. The mainstay of the programme is its daily lessons in which students are engaged in mindful attention training exercises three times a day, spending three minutes for each practice, extending to longer periods as the programme proceeds.

Two studies have been conducted on the effectiveness of MindUP. One reported on the effectiveness of the mindfulness education programme on 246 pre-adolescent and early adolescent students in the fourth to seventh grades (roughly 9 to 12 year olds; average age 11 years), drawn from six ME programme classrooms and six classrooms who did not have any training in ME (Schonert-Reichl and Lawlor, 2010). Results revealed that those who participated in the ME programme had significant increases in optimism and reported increased positive effect. Those who did not have training showed decreases in optimism. Two dimensions of teacher-rated social and emotional competence improved with the training: attention and concentration, and social emotional competence.

Pre-adolescents in the ME programme showed significant improvements in general self-concept, in contrast to those in the control group who decreased in self-concept. A slightly different picture emerged for the early adolescents in both groups, with those in the ME programme showing a decrease in general self-concept while those in the control group recorded increases in self-concept (Schonert-Reichl and Lawlor, 2010). This work suggests that there might be an optimum time period for engaging in mindfulness training and this may be before the adolescent stage. In early adolescence, there is a heightened self-consciousness due to increased competence in cognitive and social cognitive abilities and changes in information processing. These developmental changes, coupled with an intervention that fosters self-awareness, may lead to increased attention and reflection on the self, directing the early adolescent to adopt a more critical or 'realistic' view of the self (Eccles and Roeser, 2009). This work points to the timing of the intervention as a critical consideration.

The second study, also by the Schonert-Reichl team (Schonert-Reichl *et al.*, n.d.), showed that a school programme involving mindfulness and caring for others (social responsibility) enhanced cognitive control, reduced stress and produced better school outcomes. These results suggest that children's positive development can be fostered and their negative behaviours deterred via an inexpensive and easy-to-use programme delivered by regular teachers in regular elementary (in the UK primary) school classrooms.

Learning to BREATHE

Broderick and Metz (2009) directly tackled the question of mindfulness training for the more difficult adolescent period in their development of the "Learning to BREATHE" protocol for the late teens. This six-week programme aims to: increase awareness of thoughts, feelings and bodily sensations; reduce harmful self-judgements; and integrate mindful awareness into daily life. The results post-training demonstrated that, relative to students who did not undergo training, participants in the Learning to BREATHE group had increased feelings of calmness, relaxation and self-acceptance (self-compassion) and decreased negative affect. After the training, there were also improvements in emotion regulation and decreases in tiredness and aches and pains (Broderick and Metz, 2009). With adolescent groups, there is a need to ensure that the mindfulness practices are relevant and appropriate for the teen experience. Exercises that incorporate technology (e.g. phones or laptops), as well as address relevant issues (peer/social/media pressures) and take into account the fluid and intense nature of adolescent emotional experience, are advised.

Training a compassionate mind

From this developing field of mindfulness emerged interventions that brought compassion training to the fore. This includes Compassion Focused Therapy (CFT), developed by Gilbert (2010a) and Neff and Germer (2013). Gilbert defines compassion as 'a basic kindness, with a deep awareness of the suffering of oneself and of other living things, coupled with the wish and effort to relieve it' (Gilbert, 2010a, xiii, Introduction). Neff and Germer (2013: 28) define self-compassion as 'relevant to all personal experiences of suffering, including perceived inadequacies, failures, and painful life situations more generally'. In both definitions, it is clear that there is an interrelation between self and other when it comes to compassion. In order to truly understand the suffering of another, it is necessary to be intimate with our own suffering. When we become aware of and accepting of our own suffering, it is much easier to be kinder to others as they suffer. There is also an important element of action in the definition. It is not enough to just engage with the suffering alongside another; there is an active attempt to reduce the suffering, compassion being an active initiation of behaviours to reduce the suffering of ourselves or others in whatever (skilful) way is possible.

For Neff (2011), there are three main components of self-compassion: self-kindness, common humanity and mindfulness.

- *Self-kindness:* self-compassion entails being warm towards oneself when encountering pain and personal shortcomings, rather than ignoring them or hurting oneself with self-criticism.
- *Common humanity:* self-compassion also involves recognizing that suffering and personal failure is part of the shared human experience. It moves us away from the sense of isolation we feel when we think we are the only one suffering.
- *Mindfulness:* self-compassion requires taking a balanced approach to one's negative emotions so that feelings are neither suppressed nor exaggerated. Negative thoughts and emotions are observed with openness, so that they are held in mindful awareness. Mindfulness is a non-judgemental, receptive mind state during which individuals observe thoughts and feelings as they are, without trying to suppress, deny or change them. Mindfulness requires one to not be 'over-identified' with mental or emotional phenomena. This latter type of response involves narrowly focusing and ruminating on one's negative emotions.

In CFT, the objective is to help individuals to develop a sense of warmth and emotional responsiveness towards themselves as they engage in the therapeutic process (Neff and Germer, 2013). CFT accomplishes this through a variety of exercises, including visualization, as well as cultivating self-kindness through language and by engaging in self-compassionate behaviours and developing kinder habits. From the CFT approach emerged the programme modelled on MBSR called Mindful Self-Compassion (MSC), a 'hybrid' programme applicable to both the general public and to some clinical populations. The authors suggest that MSC is a complementary programme to MBSR or MBCT, since the foundations of the MSC programme rely on the prior development of skills of mindfulness.

One of the key components of the programme is the teaching of general skills of loving-kindness. This is defined as a type of friendly benevolence given to oneself in everyday situations. This might be considered as distinct from compassion, which is mainly relevant for situations involving emotional distress. Neff and Germer (2013: 31) note that MSC is considered 'a resource-building course rather than group therapy, but because self-compassion is primarily aimed at emotional suffering, the MSC programme always has two leaders, one of whom is a trained therapist for situations in which a participant requires the attention of a clinician'. A more detailed description of the programme is available at Neff and Germer (2013).

Within the educational setting, these concepts are beginning to be explored and may have particular relevance in relation to the sometimes punishing perfectionist tendencies seen in some young people.

For example, Neff, Hsieh and Dejitterat (2005) explored in two studies the relation between levels of self-compassion and academic failure. The first study showed that students with higher levels of self-compassion are better able to deal with the fear of failure and have greater perceived competence when faced with exams and general academic pressure. Confirming these findings, a second study showed that students with higher self-compassion scores are able to use more adaptive and emotionally healthy coping strategies than those with lower self-compassion levels. These studies show a direct link between the ability of students to be kind to themselves and how they manage under conditions of assessment and possible failure. In many ways, then, this training can give young people the freedom to fail – without which, no learning is possible.

Summary of research and outstanding issues

Research is ongoing with these various protocols, whether they focus on compassion or mindfulness or both. From many of these studies arises the critical question of how to support teachers in delivering mindfulness effectively. With the MindUP programme, teachers indicated that they would like to have more training themselves in mindfulness, which would allow them to explain more easily to parents what the children are doing. Early studies used a model of short intensive training to support teachers deliver the mindfulness exercises and information in the classroom. However, although teachers can easily deliver the exercises, their own experience is essential when it comes to a more in-depth understanding of the 'how and why' of mindful experience. It is relatively straightforward to deliver a mindful exercise but the real skill comes in the answers to the questions and the comments that emerge after the practices.

The issue of the teacher's own experience of mindfulness is also prevalent in discussions about the delivery of mindfulness in the health setting and this is one of the challenges of bringing this training out of the monastic setting, and into a secular one (whether a school or a healthcare setting). Looking at the four decades of healthcare research, it seems that the experience of the facilitator is a significant factor in the efficacy of a mindfulness training programme (Carmody and Baer, 2008; Khoury *et al.*, 2013). This is important when questions about the practices arise (rather than in the delivery of them *per se*). The analogy of a swimming teacher is often used. Would it be preferable to learn to swim from someone who knows a lot about swimming from reading books or from someone who can actually swim? Evidence from the mental health setting (Grepmair *et al.*, 2007) suggests that there is much to be gained even if the teachers just practise mindfulness for themselves (with no direct teaching to pupils). In this work in the mental health setting, the symptoms of patients seen by therapists who practised their own mindfulness were reduced compared with those seen by therapists who did not practise mindfulness. In this study, no mindfulness was 'taught' to the patients; only the therapists were practising for themselves. This tells us the efficacy of engaging with the practices first and foremost for ourselves.

One programme in the United States has been developed to support this process in teachers (Roeser *et al.*, 2013). The Mindfulness Training (MT) programme is an eight-week, 11-session programme with 36 contact hours. This training employs a variety of pedagogical approaches and activities designed to foster mindfulness and self-compassion as resources teachers can use to cope with stress more effectively and manifest emotional resilience more quickly. There are five main teaching activities of mindfulness and self-compassion: (i) guided mindfulness and yoga practices; (ii) group discussions of mindfulness practice; (iii) small-group activities to practise skills in real-life scenarios; (iv) lectures; and (v) home practices and homework assignments (Roeser *et al.*, 2013). Other techniques are explored during the training process, including self-compassion exercises, the development of a mindful diary, and didactic lectures. The results of this research demonstrated that 87 per cent of teachers who completed the programme found it beneficial. Teachers randomized to MT showed greater mindfulness, focused attention, working memory capacity and occupational self-compassion, as well as lower levels of occupational stress and burnout at post-programme and follow-up, compared with those in the control condition. These are encouraging results but direct evidence for how this training for teachers impacted on their ability to deliver mindfulness in the classroom is still lacking.

The literature from the clinical world, however, predicts that the programme designed by Roeser is an important step. Figure 2.3 shows the different ways that mindfulness can be employed in the school setting. In the first smallest circle, learning and using mindfulness personally as a teacher is considered the most important first step. In the second circle, the teachers and the school may begin to think about how to use mindfulness in the classroom to inform ways of working that incorporate the principles of mindfulness, and particularly a non-judgemental attitude. Lastly, the actual teaching of mindfulness to the young people directly, for example through an eight-week programme.

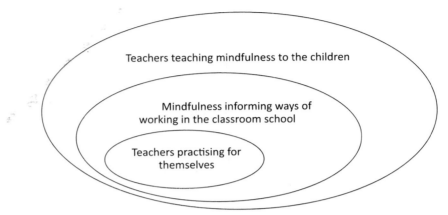

Figure 2.3: Different levels of incorporating mindfulness into the education system

One training programme currently under evaluation in a variety of settings including education, called Body in Mind Training (Russell, 2011; Russell and Tatton-Ramos, 2014), works at this second level. The invitation is to bring a mindful way of working into the classroom with some gentle teaching but mostly by focusing on the teacher's own practice and engagement with mindfulness. The schools are also encouraged to think about how their operating practices and procedures can become more mindful, thus creating the conditions within the school environment that maximize mindful and compassionate ways of being. Note that it is very difficult for a teacher to be teaching young people about kindness and compassion when what they observe is that their teacher is burnt out, exhausted and being unkind to themselves! In the next section, we will consider why it is that just being mindful and demonstrating mindfulness can be so powerful, especially in the classroom.

What happens when we observe others being mindful and compassionate?

Modelling is an essential pedagogical tool for mindfulness and compassion (Dewar and Christley, 2013; Germer, 2009) and this is especially so in the school environment. Young people are observing teachers and each other all the time and, when they see compassionate acts and compassionate ways of responding to difficult situations, this stays with them and provides a model

for their future behaviour. Th
themselves) is so essential. T
reflect the emotional tone o:
human brain to social inforn
this all of the time.

　Training in compassio
the training but there are ;
spread out into that individ
2009; Gilbert and Procter,
deliberately cultivated and e
of behaving with ourselves
When someone starts to beh
compassion) – a teacher, a c
minds in the near vicinity t∈

and compassionate states. One important neural mechanism that may underlie this ability is a system of mirror neurons that help us to interpret the mental states, intentions and affective states of others (Oztop *et al.*, 2013). The development of compassionate states is therefore a collective tool for inspiring a compassionate environment in educational institutions. As always in any organizational change, strong leadership from the headteachers and school administration supports this process.

Compassionate states of mind: Where in the brain is compassion?

The literature on brain imaging studies exploring how the brain responds following compassionate mind training is growing (Engström and Söderfeldt, 2010; Gilbert, 2010b; Immordino-Yang *et al.*, 2009; Klimecki *et al.*, 2014). In traditional Buddhist teachings, mindfulness and *metta* (or compassion) go hand in hand. This is eloquently described by Alan Wallace (Wallace and Goleman, 2006), who reminds us that training in mindfulness alone is not sufficient. We can hone our attention to a high degree but this work needs to be done alongside the development of compassionate states of mind, which will also mean that the actions arising from our mindfulness are skilful and generous. Not only that, the attention-training aspect of mindfulness also feeds into our ability to maintain a compassionate stance – the two are intimately related.

　When we look for the correlates of compassionate states of mind in the brain, we find that these are related to activity in regions that are typically associated with processing bodily sensations. These include the somatosensory cortex (where raw sensory information from and about the

or and pre-motor areas (regions preparing us
and in the world) and the insula, a region that
rmation with cognition and action and codes for
nced in the body (Holzel *et al.*, 2011; Immordino-Yang
cki *et al.*, 2014).

rior insula, particularly on the right side of the brain, seems
portant structure. This structure is thicker (Lazar *et al.*, 2005)
a greater density of grey matter in lay meditators (Holzel *et al.*,
. In a structural neuroimaging study by Luders *et al.* (2012), cortial
rification in the right anterior insula was positively correlated with years
of practice of meditation. This imaging method looks at how much the
brain folds over inside the skull and works on the assumption that, if the
brain grows (as a result of mindfulness practice), then it will fold over more
as the skull limits the amount by which it can grow outwards. These studies
suggest that there is something fundamentally different about the insular
cortex in those people who meditate as the more meditation practice that is
carried out, the greater the changes in this brain region.

What would happen if you had a denser or larger insular cortex? One
hypothesis is that you would be able to feel more: you would have greater
sensitivity to bodily sensations of different sorts, including those related to
emotional states (Sze *et al.*, 2010). This is important as genuine compassion
for others can only come from the ability to tolerate and be compassionate
towards our own suffering. This ability comes when we can tolerate and not
react to even difficult sensations or emotions in our own bodies. Thus our
ability to hone our own emotional intelligence has a direct impact on how
we relate emotionally to others.

In functional brain imaging studies of compassion training. much
of the work has come from studies looking at experts in compassion,
often monks (Lutz *et al.*, 2008). One study asked participants (monks and
laypeople) to engage in a practice where they thought of an individual who
was dear to them and then wished wholeheartedly for that person to be free
from suffering (Lutz *et al.*, 2008). This is a typical practice for compassion
training from the Buddhist tradition. Comparing the monks to those who
had only one week of this compassion training, the results showed that
a region of the right insular cortex was more active in the monks. In this
study, they probed the brain with a task requiring subjects to listen to
negative sounds. It was under these conditions that the monks had a great
activation of the brain in the right insula. This activation was related to
years of meditation practice: the more you practise, the more activation in
the right insula to negative sounds.

How does this finding relate to our life and compassion in the classroom? The key finding here is that we wish to help and support our young people to be able to cope when things go wrong. They will certainly find times in their lives when they are experiencing strong emotions, such as fear and loss, and they will meet with frustrations on a day-to-day basis. This training does not make these realities of life disappear. Rather, it provides the tools with which to ensure that, even when these things occur, we do not have to be overwhelmed by them. Because we are not overwhelmed, we maintain the capacity to think clearly, and also think of others in the situation. In a way that takes multiple perspectives into account, we have less tunnel vision and greater ability to problem-solve in that situation.

Another well-designed functional imaging study (Klimecki *et al.*, 2014) explored some key differences between an increased empathic versus compassionate mode of responding. This study used healthy female participants who underwent a short empathy training protocol and then subsequently a compassion training protocol. The results showed that there were distinct patterns of behavioural and neural response to the two types of training. While empathy training increased activation in regions related to emotional experience such as the insula cortex bilaterally (and with associated increases in negative affect), these patterns were reversed after the compassion training. The authors interpreted these results as indicating that empathy (feeling along with someone) may not be helpful and may lead to burnout, whereas training in compassion reverses these effects. The compassion training leaves the individual with the chance to engage more skilfully and in a more sustainable way with the suffering of others, while also looking after themselves. This is vital for those who work in professions requiring care of others (Russell, 2014). Note that this study used meditation-naïve participants who underwent a short training (not monks with years of training).

Summary and take-home message/activity

In summary, mindfulness and compassion are intimately linked. We train our attention but the quality of the attention (open, accepting, kind) is equally important. A growing evidence base indicates that mindfulness training has good efficacy across a range of settings, age groups and with a variety of programmes. Some specific compassion training programmes also exist but these are less well evaluated in populations of young people or educational settings.

In the brain, when experts generate compassionate states of mind, the regions of the brain that code for our bodily reactions are activated, suggesting that we do have that embodied sense of another's suffering but are able to tolerate this in a way that means we can still think clearly. When individuals are trained in this way, they can be *more* open to the suffering of others. What seems clear from this work is that those who wish to teach mindfulness in the educational setting must first practise mindfulness for themselves. This will not only ensure that their teaching is authentic but will also allow them to be better able to explain the concepts in the classroom. The starting point is a connection to our own suffering and unruly minds in a genuine, open and curious way and, through this, being able to communicate gently that we all share these same experiences.

Ten things I can do right now

1. Stop and pause when I notice I am feeling a strong emotion.

2. Drop into the body and pay attention to any feeling states.

3. Take time to acknowledge emotions in the classroom in a neutral and curious way.

4. Take time to care for your body – it's a highly tuned instrument.

5. Check your posture periodically, is there enough 'space' in the torso for emotions to be freely felt?

6. Introduce mindfulness language around emotions in the classroom. Replace 'I am angry' with a description of what is going on in the body (tightening, clenching).

7. Work with the children to develop a language of emotions in the body.

8. Visit www.wired.co.uk/news/archive/2014-01/02/mapping-body-emotions to read up on the bodily sensations of emotional states.

9. Create a 'body barometer' in the classroom to start to label the different sensations that are associated with different emotions.

10. Reinforce at every opportunity that we all feel the same sensations when we are sad, lonely, angry, frustrated or happy, excited and joyful.

Chapter 3

BE ORACLES POWER: Compassion though spiritual development

Maurice Irfan Coles

> *We had the experience but missed the meaning.*
> (T.S. Eliot, 'The Dry Salvages', from *Four Quartets*)

Abstract

One could say that without compassion there is no spirituality. One could equally argue, however, that without spirituality compassion would not exist, for compassion forms the bedrock of spiritual practice. Compassion and spirituality are interwoven and integral. The same is true of the social and moral dimensions of education, all of which could be subsumed under 'the spiritual'. Indeed, the compassionate school will, almost by definition, be a school promoting spiritual development. Words, however, are slippery and, to become meaningful, require careful definition. This chapter unpacks the terms 'spirit', 'spirituality', 'spiritual' and 'spiritual development' and explores their relationship to compassion. It defines spiritual development as perspective, process and content; and provides a detailed taxonomy employing the mnemonic *BE ORACLES POWER*, which aims to encapsulate spiritual development's essential characteristics as well as offering schools a simple aide-memoire. It provides a range of spiritual signposts, which educators can take into their own settings. The chapter is designed to help begin to ground the practice of spirituality into teaching and learning experiences that are readily understood by all and can be translated into the language of the classroom, thereby making spiritual experiences for young people an everyday lived reality.

Introduction

Have you ever met a person who has never had a spiritual experience, who has never asked questions about the nature and point of existence? 'Where did I come from?' is one of young children's first meaningful questions. As they grow and get a sense of the wider world, they ask about meaning and purpose, about the causes of suffering and death, and about their identity and place in the world. Scratch the surface of many adults and they will own to having some experience and awareness of the transcendent, of the synchronistic, and of some often inexplicable force that is greater than themselves. The issue for many people, however, is that they have no effective means of processing, interpreting and learning from these events; in the words of T.S. Eliot, 'We had the experience but missed the meaning.' It is partly the function of education to help young people to explore the greater meaning of their experiences, to provide a vocabulary to aid understanding and to offer curricular opportunities for further development and exploration.

Once discussion of these issues starts, however, we come up against the problems and limitations of language, for so many of our perceptions of spirituality are conditioned by the language and cultural assumptions of the society and the age in which we live. Yet the language of spirit permeates our culture. We seek spiritual leaders and want to find our *spiritual home*. We talk of 'a person of *spirit*' or 'the *spirit* of 45'. We say, by way of encouragement, 'That's the *spirit*!' and when a person is defeated and deflated we say, 'they have lost their *spirit*'. But ask people to define what they mean by 'spirit' and 'spiritual' and they struggle.

Returning to the root of the word 'spirit' might help. Interestingly, whether in English, Greek, Latin, Sanskrit, Arabic or Hebrew, the words for spirit and spiritual all share a common derivation, regardless of language – they all come from the word for *breath*. The English *spirit* means 'animating or vital principle in humans and animals', and stems from the Old French *espirit*, which in turn comes from the Latin word *spiritus*, 'soul, courage, vigour, breath'. Its root is *spirare*, 'to breathe', from which we derive words such as inspire (which originally meant under the immediate influence of God or a god), aspire and even conspire (which meant 'to breathe together', even if it was for some secret nefarious purpose). The Greek *pneuma*, Hebrew *ruah* and Arabic *ruh* all share the dual meaning of spirit and breath. Even the Sanskrit for soul, self, spirit – *atman* – derives from the word for breath.

Spirit and soul are often used as synonyms, although one might argue that soul has religious connotations whereas spirit can be more secular as it is a universal human trait. We are less clear about the etymology of the word 'soul'. It is thought that it derives from the Old English *sawol* meaning 'spiritual and emotional part of a person, animate existence; life, living being'. The word is probably an adaptation by early missionaries of a Germanic concept, which was a translation of Greek *psyche*, 'life, spirit, consciousness', which is derived from the verb 'to cool, to blow' and hence refers to the vital breath, the animating principle in humans and other animals. Put simply, we breathe therefore we are spiritual; being human is being a spiritual being. Or, put another way, in the words of the French philosopher, scientist and theologian, Pierre Teilhard de Chardin (1955), 'We are not human beings having a spiritual experience; we are spiritual beings having a human experience.'

Understanding the universal origin of the word and appreciating its cognate linguistic connections is a beginning, but we still lack clear definition as to the essential characteristics of spirituality. In the certain knowledge that any definition is bound to attract criticism from philosophers and theorists, we must nevertheless attempt to offer a working definition and then ground it in a teaching reality; must translate it from the language of speculative theorists to the language of classroom practitioners and curriculum designers.

The characteristics of spirituality: The existential and the collective; the active and the contemplative; the sacred and the secular

Spirituality is one of those portmanteau terms that do not lend themselves to exact definition or clear delineated boundaries. For educators, grappling to transform it into classroom practice is both a beauty and a torment. It is a beauty because it permits exciting creativity and leaps of imagination; but it can also be a torment because 'spirituality' appears so difficult to translate for the classroom. As you try to define it, you realize its complexities and its elusive and ineffable qualities. An extensive review of literature, however, does reveal some general areas of agreement. As we shall see, spirituality relates to three overarching complementary clusters: the existential and the collective; the active and the contemplative; and the sacred and the secular. The key to them all is that each experience has the power to transform the individual in one way or another; each can help young people to reach heights and articulate sentiments that may initially have appeared to be beyond their grasp.

Spirituality can be viewed as the journey towards ultimate reality, which gives our life meaning and purpose. It is existential in that the experience is unique to each individual. For Brother Wayne Teasdale in *The Mystic Heart* (1999: 10), spirituality 'refers to an individual solitary search for the discovery of the absolute or the divine'. For him, this can involve direct mystical experience of the transcendent, which requires practices that act as a conduit to inner change and growth. All humans, he argues, have this mystical capacity, the capacity for direct immediate experience of the ultimate reality, whatever language and cultural constructs one uses to describe it. Others, like the authors of the *Vedanta* in the Hindu traditions, speak of self-realization (*atma-jnana*), by which they mean knowledge of the 'true' self beyond delusion and beyond the world of matter: knowledge that they maintain leads the individual to the path of selfless love. Similarly, expressed in secular terms, Abraham Maslow and Carl Rogers, leaders in the humanistic psychology movement, refer to 'self-actualization', which forms the pinnacle of Maslow's hierarchy of needs (Maslow, 1954). Self-actualization is the awakening and manifestation of latent potentialities of the human being in areas like the aesthetic, the ethical, the religious and the spiritual. Maslow also referred to self-transcendence, which could lead to 'peak experiences', moments of intense joy, wonder, awe and ecstasy, after which people could be inspired, strengthened, renewed or transformed (Maslow, 1964).

Although primarily personal, spirituality is played out in the collective and has moral, social and cultural dimensions. How we articulate our own identity is fashioned by the society in which we live and its dominant values. Thus, for example, children from a Hindu or Sikh or secular background are likely to express their spirituality in different ways, according to how they have been brought up and the dominant narratives of their respective communities. Wright (cited in Eaude, 2008: 15) argues that 'spirituality is the relationship of the individual, within community and tradition, to that which is – or is perceived to be – of ultimate concern, of ultimate value, and ultimate truth, as appropriate through an informed, sensitive and reflective striving for spiritual wisdom.'

It is through the dynamic relationship of the individual and the community that our spirituality is expressed. It exists both inside us and between the people with whom we interact. This interaction is described by David Hay and Rebecca Nye in *The Spirit of the Child* (2006) as 'relational consciousness', which includes four broad dual-patterned sets: the I-Self, the I-Others, the I–World and the I–God. Their research discovered that a spiritual dimension is a latent part of all humans, whether or not they are religious. It appears that even the very young search for this wider relationship with the transcendent: asking questions of deep philosophic meaning, trying to locate themselves in the wider world and beginning to contemplate the mysteries of life.

The contemplative has traditionally been associated with spirituality. In common usage, 'contemplate' means to think deeply, to ponder, to admire. It derives from the Latin *contemplatio*, which has *templum* as its root: a piece of consecrated ground or a building for worship. In a religious and spiritual sense, contemplation is usually a type of prayer or meditation. The contemplative ideal is admirable and there are those who renounce the world to spend their time reflecting upon the nature of God. For many religious traditions, the state of our world is so parlous that retiring from the world is no longer seen as a viable option and active engagement with societal problems is now seen as the order of the day. Prayer and meditation may form the contemplative foundation, but social action is the necessary corollary.

There are those who argue that spirituality needs to be lived and active in order to become fully realized. In *The Practical Visionary: A new world guide to spiritual growth and social change* (2010: 3), Corinne McLaughlin argues that 'while vision essentially comes from the spiritual dimension within you, being practical is focusing on what's needed, appropriate and timely when applying your vision'. For her, the practical dimension is just as sacred as the visionary. David Hay makes a similar link. In the preface to the first edition of *The Spirit of the Child* (Hay and Nye, 2006: 9), he argues, 'Rather surprisingly, spiritual education has become newsworthy.' 'One major reason for this', he continues, 'is a growing public concern about the coherence of society as a whole, allied to an intuition that spirituality has importance in maintaining what Philip Selznick calls the moral commonwealth.' For Hay, the most important single finding of his research over 30 years is the very strong connection found between spiritual awareness and ethical behaviour. People link their spiritual or religious experience with a moral imperative. Hay maintains that children are capable of profound, meaningful beliefs from an early age, despite cultural pressures and the decline of institutional religion, and makes the case for spirituality as a means of fostering morality and social inclusion.

Morality, social inclusion and coherence are all heavily value-laden terms open to differing interpretations. These interpretations are in turn linked to our culture, our particular way of seeing the world. They all imply value judgements that are based upon what we believe, what we hold to be of ultimate importance: the moral compass upon which we set our direction of travel. If, for example, we believe that selfless service and collaboration rather than individualism and wealth acquisition are our key values, then this will influence how we behave towards other people, how we set our goals and how we live our lives. Spirituality and morality are inextricably linked because they both relate to how we see ourselves, what we hold to be of fundamental importance and what we consider most sacred in our lives.

The notion of sacred is similarly culturally connected. The word itself originally comes from the Latin *sacrum*, which referred to the gods or anything in their power, and to *sacerdos* (priest) and *sanctum*, which meant set apart. Colloquially, we talk of sacred as something we hold to be holy, something that is blessed, and something we want to protect and revere; something that, literally, makes us whole. Paradoxically, these can be found in areas traditionally described as secular. Sportsmen and women talk of the 'sacred turf', of inhabiting 'a zone' that transports them out of themselves, of being 'in the flow' that makes them the complete athlete. The psychologists who developed the concept of flow acknowledge their debt to various spiritual and religious practices wherein participants immerse themselves in a physical task and channel their total being in the service of their chosen activity. When people are 'in flow', emotions are energized and aligned with the task at hand. Participants report a feeling of spontaneous joy, even rapture, while on task.

Similarly, participants in a project dedicated to exploring 'sacred spaces' with young people' (Coles and Scoble, 2012: 3) agreed that a sacred space could be 'simply anywhere'. It was not necessarily faith dependent and existed in architecture, in nature, in art sculpture and stained glass, in all types of music, in literature and storytelling, in symbols and imagery, ritual and prayer. Such places, they went on, can exist in the public and private domains, can be part of our communal areas and part of our homes and gardens. The sacred is not a different kingdom but it is an awareness that can pervade any area of life. It is a perception that takes us out of ourselves and transports us from the mundane to the extraordinary.

When you talk of the 'sacred' and the 'spiritual', many people automatically associate this with religion and faith groups, seeing them as largely exclusive conduits though which the spirit flows. Faith groups are major – but not exclusive – conduits and, whether they originate from India (Hinduism, Buddhism and Sikhism), China (Confucianism and Daoism) or the Near East (Judaism, Christianity and Islam), it could be argued that, in spite of their many nuances, they share common spiritual beliefs:

- that spiritual knowledge is obtainable
- that all humanity is one and is inextricably connected to the natural world
- that we must have compassion and respect for all and must follow the Golden Rule of treating everybody as we would wish to be treated.

Despite many doctrinal, sectarian and creedal differences that can divide them, there appears to be a growing understanding that the major religions are joined at the heart and that they share kindred pathways through compassion. This spiritual awareness of Oneness (Vaughan-Lee, 2002), of the interconnectivity of faith traditions, is mirrored in the secular sphere by the realization that our planet is one and that what happens in one part of it will have an impact elsewhere; that the world is now our backyard and, hence, is our collective and shared responsibility. Llewellyn Vaughan-Lee, a teacher in the Naqshbandiyya-Mujaddidiyya Sufi order, has written extensively on spiritual responsibility in this time of global crises and on what he terms 'spiritual ecology'(Vaughan-Lee, 2013b). His son, Emmanuel, has produced two remarkable films on these issues, both of which come with guidance notes for teachers. The first, *One – the movie: A contemporary journey towards a timeless destiny* (2012), graphically underlines the commonalities in people of faith and spirit, with contributions from a range of theologians and mystics from all faith backgrounds (*see* Vaughan-Lee, n.d.(a)). The second, *Elemental* (2015), tells the story of three individuals united by their deep connection with nature and driven to confront some of the most pressing ecological challenges of our time (*see* Vaughan-Lee, n.d.(b)).

With the decline of religious observance, however, many people talk of being spiritual but not religious; of owning to a spiritual drive without a creedal base. The enormous success of James Redfield's *The Celestine Prophecy* (1993), his subsequent books, overarching vision and worldwide movement, are testimony to the people who stress *spirit without faith*. For Redfield, the key to our spiritual future lies in the conscious development of synchronicity, of those seemingly coincidental and serendipitous events that we all experience; coincidences that sometimes lead us to take another step in our personal journey. For example, how often have we been thinking of a person and the phone rings; or troubling over a major decision and we read or meet or hear something which helps us to resolution? Though the concept is referred to in the *Vedantas*, the Swiss psychologist Carl Jung was the first modern thinker to define this phenomenon as synchronicity, 'the perception of meaningful coincidence'. Jung maintained that synchronicity was an acausal principle in the universe, a law that operated to move human beings towards greater growth in consciousness. Synchronicity can be related to intuition, to sudden insights, to a feeling that one should take a particular action or follow a particular path. Colloquially, we talk of an inner wisdom, and there are countless examples of thinkers, scientists and artists who, facing a seemingly insurmountable challenge, slept, dreamt, meditated upon or suddenly envisioned a solution that appeared beyond their rational mind.

Meditation and yoga are two key vehicles for strengthening this intuition and inner wisdom. Meditation and contemplative prayer have always been key features of the world's great religions. More recently, however, the secular mindfulness movement has become a mainstay of much psychological and educational practice. Whether secular or faith based, meditation techniques share much in common in that they all try to still the mind, all practise following the breath, often chant a repeated phrase and recommend meditation as regular practice. There are, however, many different types of meditation and many ways of expressing them. McLaughlin (2010: 175), for example, lists six kinds: concentration, contemplation, mindfulness, receptive meditation, creative mediation and invocation. Whatever the taxonomy used, neuroscientific research offers clear evidence of its benefits. Scientists have found that meditation creates enduring gamma rays that not only alter the brain but increase the positivity, happiness, heightened perceptions and insights of the meditator. Similarly, meditation causes changes in the physiological structure of the brain by increasing cognitive and emotional processing and a sense of well-being. According to McLaughlin, more than 600 scientific studies in the classroom have verified that 10–15 minutes of meditation twice a day improves students' achievement, reduces stress, promotes creativity and decreases substance abuse. Meditation is not simply an existential act. It has traditionally also been practised in groups and now, increasingly, groups are using social media to come together at the same time across the globe to meditate upon a particular cause or theme.

In the last quarter-century, we have learned more about how the brain works than in the preceding two millennia. This knowledge has caused us to question the nature of intelligence itself and the nature of the learning process. The old IQ (intelligence quotient) theories have given way to more sophisticated analyses about different types of intelligence and how educators can nurture them. In his seminal book about multiple intelligences, and subsequent works, Howard Gardner (1983) argues that there are at least seven kinds of intelligence, including musical, spatial and sporting, as well as rational and emotional. In the mid-1990s, Daniel Goleman popularized research from a range of neuroscientists and psychologists when he argued that emotional intelligence was as important as rational intelligence and the other intelligences (Goleman, 1996). Zohar and Marshall (2000) go further and maintain that there is a further and ultimate intelligence, spiritual intelligence. The search for meaning, for answers to the ultimate questions, was one of the prime movers in the development of language, the symbolic imagination and the growth of the human brain. The authors cite recent neurological research in support of their contention that each of us is born with and can develop what they call 'the spiritual quotient'.

There is some research in the UK context that examines the role of faith and spirit in the lives of young people. The work of Eleanor Nesbitt has over time provided valuable insights. Her chapter on spirituality and religious experience in *Intercultural Education, Ethnographic and Religious Approach* (2004), for example, examines the spiritual experiences of young Christians, Hindus and Sikhs. The most comprehensive work we have on this subject is *Urban Hope and Spiritual Health: The Adolescent Voice* by Leslie J. Francis and Mandy Robbins (2005). This study had its origins in the Commission on Urban Life and Faith, which was established to mark the twentieth anniversary of Faith in the City (1985).

It also built upon the report *Spiritual Health and the Well Being of Urban Young People* (Rees, Francis and Robbins, 2005). Over 23,000 students from Years 9 and 10 in urban schools were interviewed for the study. As the Church of England reported in February 2006, under the headline, 'Faith plays a part in health of teenagers': 'Young people with no faith have such low self-esteem that one in four have contemplated suicide and teenagers who belong to a faith community were much more likely to feel that their life had a sense of purpose.' The authors prefer the construct 'spiritual health', to 'spiritual development' or 'religion', partly because they found 'spiritual development' too imprecise a term for their study and partly because the place of religion in England and Wales is both contested and ambiguous. For them, spiritual health is a third of a triad: physical health, mental health and spiritual health. For Leslie Francis, 'spiritual health is about relationships. Good spiritual health is reflected in four areas: good relationship with self, good relationship with others, good relationship with the environment, good relationship with the transcendent.' This is remarkably similar to Hay and Nye's theory (2006) of relational consciousness discussed above. Spirit may indeed be the breath of life and be fundamental to our well-being, but educators need to know and understand how this can be translated to the classroom and be developed in school settings.

The characteristics of spiritual development: Perspective, process and content

Since 1944, at least in England and Wales, the terminology of the 1944 Education Act has assumed a critical significance in that it requires that all state maintained schools 'promote the spiritual development of pupils and of society'. It was probably true to say, however, that outside schools with a religious character, the legislation was *more* honoured *in the breach than* in *the observance*. This situation dramatically altered in 1988, however, with the introduction of 'spiritual development' as one of the key criteria in regular systematic school inspections. Almost overnight, schools had to grapple with not only an understanding of what spiritual development meant, but also with its practical classroom application. They were helped by the publication of guidance from the inspection regime, Ofsted (Office for Standards in Education), and by several publications from various non-statutory government bodies like the former School Curriculum and Asssessment Authority (SCAA) and latterly the Qualifications and Curriculum Authority (QCA), which aimed to help schools navigate the spiritual maze. Coles (2007), in his *Faith, Interfaith and Cohesion*, and Martin Rawle's web-based PhD thesis (2011) both chart the detailed discussions of this evolving concept.

QCA (1997), for example, employing some of the language of self-actualization, argued that to promote pupils' spiritual development is to actively encourage 'the growth of pupils' inner life, their capacity to relate to others and their non-material well-being for example their self-respect – their creativity, their will to achieve their full potential and their ability to try and find answers to life's major questions, including the existence and nature of God'. It emphasized the importance of spiritual development for all pupils, not only for those with religious beliefs: 'Those who believe in God will understand spiritual development differently from those who do not. But spiritual development is independent of religious belief. It is the entitlement of all pupils and the responsibility of all adults. Given the link between development of the human spirit and human motivation, the promotion of pupils' spiritual development is a vital part of school life.' Similarly, Ofsted over time has provided detailed and helpful guidance for schools and inspectors in which they list characteristics of pupils who are developing spiritually; and relate these to what schools might be doing to encourage such development (for example, *see* Ofsted, 2004).

On the basis of Ofsted and QCA descriptors, meditation, wider reading and discussion, a detailed taxonomy employing the mnemonic *BE ORACLES POWER* has been developed. This aims to encapsulate spiritual development's essential characteristics while offering schools an aide-memoire. Interestingly, the mnemonic itself resonates spiritually. 'Be', in its active imperative form, relates to being and appears eight times in the Qu'ran as a commandment from God for the Universe and Man to come into existence. 'Oracles' derives from the latin *orare* meaning to speak, pray and plead, and in many cultures oracles were seen as voices from the sky or messages from the gods. 'Power' relates to the countless examples of forces that can accompany spiritual beings on their quest for truth.

The descriptors themselves are predicated upon the contention that spiritual development is essentially a perspective, an attitude, a way of seeing, hearing, thinking and feeling about the world. If teachers employ this perspective in their thinking and planning, if they utilize the characteristics upon which this perspective is based effectively, they will help their pupils develop spiritually. The compassionate processes they adopt as role models in their teaching styles, the opportunities they afford for pupils to challenge, ask the big questions, and make the connections, help to ground this development.

BE ORACLES POWER: A TAXONOMY OF SPIRITUAL DEVELOPMENT

Pupils who are growing spiritually are likely to be developing an understanding and appreciation of some of the following:

Beauty and the Big picture
Ecology and Environment

Oneness and the Ow factor
Ritual and Relationships
Awe, Awareness and Appreciation
Childlike qualities, Charity, Compassion and Creativity
Love, Laughter and Listening
Enthusiasm
Sacred, Silence, Stewardship and Service

Peace, Principles, Purpose and Prayer
Openness
Wonder and the Wow factor
Emotional literacy
Reflection and Respect

Parts of this taxonomy have been explained earlier in this chapter; others are self-explanatory; some require brief further clarification here.

Beauty: Notions of beauty are generally culturally specific and young people need to be taught how to 'read' beauty, how to appreciate, for example, the glories of the world's buildings and art. Although Christopher Wren argued that 'architecture aims at eternity', it is probably only in the glories of nature that there appears to be universal agreement. The poets express it best. None better perhaps than the English mystic poet, William Blake, when he urged us 'To see a World in a Grain of Sand / And a Heaven in a Wild Flower, / Hold Infinity in the palm of your hand / And Eternity in an hour' ('Auguries of Innocence').

The Big picture is the capacity to see beyond the confines of one's own time and culture. It is about the big spiritual questions of life and how humans perceive them.

The Ow factor is the antidote to the 'wow' factor (sometimes also referred to as 'awe and wonder'), to the tendency of teachers to stress the many positives of our and others' spiritual peak experiences, without dealing with the darker shadow side of existence like the causes of suffering, death and decay, injustice and unfairness, or the fact that even the best of people sometimes do bad things.

Ritual has a Latin derivation, *ritus*, which means a custom or way of doing something. We all inhabit a world of ritual at school and at home, as we grow and age. It is part of the human condition and it serves a unique function, providing some constancy and space in a fast-moving frenetic world. 'In the space that ritual provides for', writes Tony Buzan (2001), 'you can become more involved in the thoughts and actions that allow you to enter more fully into your spiritual being.'

Awe involves a sense of wonder at events bigger than oneself. It might entail reverence, esteem, veneration, even worship. This sense of awe can sometimes evoke key moments of insight, epiphanies that can transform the life of an individual.

Awareness includes the importance of intuition, of insight that sometimes helps us to see beyond the rational and logical.

Appreciation includes thankful acknowledgement of the intangible, of the bigger concepts like beauty, truth and love as well as the mystery of life.

Childlike qualities: Buzan (2001) lists ten qualities that children possess, including unconditional love, trust, energy and enthusiasm. These make children 'natural' exponents of what he calls spiritual intelligence. He argues that, in order to boost our own spirituality, we would do well to observe and learn from them.

Compassion: The CoED Foundation, after considerable research, agreed that 'love in action' was the simplest and most accessible definition of compassion but over 30 characteristics of a compassionate person were identified as underpinning this definition. Compassion is simply expressed and easily understood. It acts as a unifying meta-value that young people can make an everyday lived reality by following the Golden Rule. It is, in the words of Michael Fullan (2001), all about 'relationships, relationships, relationships'.

Laughter: 'Laughter', wrote actor and humorist Peter Ustinov, 'is the most civilised music in the world.' All available evidence points to its wonderful properties in progressing our health, wealth and overall happiness. Laughter offers a perspective that at once defuses tensions and conflict and leaves the other feeling valued. People of great spiritual power, like the present Dalai Lama and Archbishop Tutu, still have the power to make us laugh. Others, like Nelson Mandela and Mahatma Gandhi, had a well-developed sense of humour and fun and were well aware of the power this carried. As Gandhi put it, 'If I had no sense of humour, I would long ago have committed suicide.' But he cautioned about the dangers of laughing at people rather than laughing with them, saying about the British Empire, 'First they ignore you, then they laugh at you, then they fight you, then you win.' The great American sociologist Peter L. Berger, in his book *Redeeming Laughter* (2014), points to how both laughter and religion have a transcendental quality in that they enable us to stand outside everyday experience. Even Ofsted, in its list of spiritual criteria, uses the verb 'enjoy'.

Listening: '*If we were supposed to talk more than we listen, we would have two tongues and one ear,*' wrote the American author and wit Mark Twain. Yet listening is a much undervalued skill in our education system, although it is fundamental to spiritual development because it helps the listener to understand the other and to be more compassionate towards them. The technique of 'active listening', of being able to listen and then feed back what has been heard to the speaker, by way of re-stating or paraphrasing, is an invaluable technique that permits greater understanding and can help in conflict resolution. The power of 'inner listening', the technique of remaining silent and going into the heart in order to develop intuition, is much more difficult to translate into educational practice. Various meditative schools encourage this to enable the individual to think deeply on an issue of major concern and receive guidance by way of intuition.

Silence: Our children are bombarded by constant noise, by constant demands on them to be successful, to have a market-driven body image, to eat and dress in a certain way, to listen to a particular type of music and so on. Silence is seldom part of young people's lives yet it is key to deeper and more intuitive understanding. Increasingly, schools are trying to provide a time for silence; a time to slow the pace without the constant barrage of noise.

Stewardship of each other, and of the planet in all its diversity, is key not only to all major religions but also to humanists and other secular groups, and it leads directly to the virtue of **Service**; of helping altruistically.

Prayer can be a contentious issue in schools and society and, like religious observance, appears to have declined over the years. People of faith and many of spirit believe in its efficacy, however. In *How Do You Pray?* (2014), Celeste Yacoboni has collected a fascinating collection of 'inspiring responses from religious leaders, spiritual guides, healers, activists and other lovers of humanity'. For her, 'the way we pray provides a mirror to our soul. It reflects our most fundamental values and beliefs, hopes and dreams, fears and doubts. Prayer unifies us with ourselves and with each other by putting us in touch with the divine essence within' (xvi).

Emotional literacy is not a new notion but its profile was significantly enhanced in 1995 (1996 in the UK) following the release of Daniel Goleman's book, *Emotional Intelligence: Why it can matter more than IQ*, and his subsequent work has further enhanced this profile. A study of the literature reveals that there are many different formulations and definitions of emotional literacy but they might usefully be broken down into five key interdependent components:

- self-awareness, that is, a reflective state that acts as the main foundation for the development of the other four elements
- self-regulation
- empathy and compassion
- social skills, which can be divided into interpersonal (what you need for effective relationship management) and intra-personal (what you need for effective self-management)
- motivation, that which drives an individual to succeed in life. Self-motivation, in conjunction with the other areas of emotional literacy, assists in achieving difficult goals and succeeding against the odds.

Reflection: 'Men go abroad to wonder at the height of the mountains, at the huge waves of the sea, at the long course of the rivers, at the vast compass of the oceans, at the circular motion of the stars; and they pass by themselves without wondering' (St Augustine of Hippo).

One of the most important skills we can give young people is the skill of critical reflection, both of their inner feelings, experiences and behaviours and of the feelings and behaviours of others. This is crucial to their emotional and spiritual development and is an aim shared by humanistic psychology and by all major religious traditions and by many major civilizations. Like compassion, 'know thyself' is axiomatic to self-realization and to self-actualization. For the Greeks, *gnōthi seauton* ('know thyself') was inscribed in the forecourt of the Temple of Apollo at Delphi. The Roman aphorism *nosce te ipsum* held the same meaning. For many religions, self-knowledge leads to knowledge of God. In Islam, one of the hadith (reported sayings of the prophet Muhammad), 'He who Knows himself knows His Lord', leads to *muhasabah*, critical self-knowledge. Hindus talk of *Atmanam Viddhi*, which steers us to the realization that we are all aspects of the divine. For the Buddhists, 'All change comes from within'.

BE ORACLES POWER offers a useful aide-memoire for schools to evaluate their existing provision, but schools are beleaguered institutions with a huge weight of societal expectation upon them to produce ever higher exam grades. They require guidance and exemplar materials to support them in providing adequate pathways to spiritual development. The stark truth appears to be that, although we have much scholarly writing on the subject, especially in publications like the *International Journal of Children's Spirituality*, we have far fewer recorded examples of effective guidance and best practice.

Spiritual signposts: Pathways to spiritual development

'There is no simple set of instructions on how to proceed … it is a way of going about things, and it demands the courage to breathe moral and spiritual motivation into everything, to seek the human dimension in all things. Science, technology, expertise, and so-called professionalism are not enough. Something more is necessary. For the sake of simplicity, it might be called spirit. Or feeling. Or Conscience' (Havel, 1992, n.p.).

Although this poet, playwright and president was reflecting on the nature of democracy, his eloquent statement can be applied to spiritual development. Teachers and school managers are, however, hampered by a lack of instructions, by the dearth of best practice examples that can be adapted to their own circumstances, and by a poverty of conceptual understanding and training in the spiritual. In our current system, we value what we can measure and record publicly, and spiritual development slips down the hierarchy of importance because we cannot effectively measure it. Yet, it is probably true to say that many schools exhibit what Maslow has called, 'unconscious competence'; that is, without actually realizing it, schools are helping young people to develop many of the characteristics outlined in BE ORACLES POWER. They may well have the necessary perspective, 'the way of going about things', and the courage already, but it is rarely systematically applied and is therefore at real risk of being lost.

The Royal Society of Arts' excellent report on spiritual, moral, social and cultural provision, *Schools with Soul* (2014), highlights many schools' strengths in providing for these areas but argues that spiritual development is the most neglected. Their research indicates that schools are undertaking spiritual development as a cross-curricular initiative, which they build into their whole-school, medium- and short-term planning. Although many schools – and not just those with a religious character – could point to some good practice, it is probably true to say that there is generally no coherent overview, no systematic implementation of the underlying principles that have been built into planning. So provision becomes scatter-gun or haphazard in approach, relying more on the individual teacher's passion than planned policy implementation.

Recently, there has been an exponential growth in the number of schools undertaking meditation classes, whether Christian, Buddhist, Hindu, transcendental or, by far the most popular, mindfulness. In addition, many schools are discovering the benefits of yoga for their pupils. Schools are employing the materials developed to stimulate learning about such things as 'forgiveness' and 'sacred spaces'. Much excellent work has been undertaken in the field of interfaith teaching, especially – but not exclusively – in the teaching of religious education. The social and emotional aspects of spirituality are particularly well supported, with significant initiatives such as the comprehensive Department for Education (DfE) programme, Social and Emotional Aspects of Learning (SEAL). Lessons related to conflict resolution and the teaching of controversial issues are available from the Religious Education Council's REsilience project and from organizations such as the Forgiveness Project. Similarly, much of the material used in character, human scale and values education promotes spiritual development.

The issue, however, is that young people are not developing a suitable language of spirituality, a language to help them understand and interpret the meaning of their experiences. Spirituality is 'caught' and not taught, which is probably why, both here and in the United States, teenagers associate it with religion. Materials are available that cover spirituality more discretely but these are not school specific and require adaptation. There is a wealth of literature concerning spiritual and religious paths but it is not the function of secular schools to recommend any one.

Conclusion: Spiritual development, compassion and schools

Spiritual development for pupils and staff involves the cultivation of a perspective, an attitude, and a way of seeing the world, each other and the curriculum as a vehicle for connecting us to a deeper reality that animates and sustains us. It requires the conscious classroom implementation of a number of key characteristics that will support young people in the development of their identity, self-worth and understanding of life's ultimate meaning and purpose. It will enhance their interconnectivity, their sense of the 'sacred', and sharpen their understanding of the responsibilities they will bear for the future. It can be accessed directly and indirectly through cross-curricular activities, subject-specific initiatives and project-focused work. It overlaps with social, moral and cultural development and is based on compassion.

So what would a school look like that was promoting spiritual development? We have taken Ofsted's very useful list (2004; shown within quotation marks) as our baseline, and added to it. Schools that are encouraging pupils' spiritual development are, therefore, likely to:

- be clear about the aims and characteristics of spiritual development and how they impact upon the curriculum and young people
- be explicit in their values, moral purpose and compassionate ethos
- actively encourage experiences that help young people transcend their own cultural backgrounds
- provide opportunities 'to explore values and beliefs, including religious beliefs, and the way in which they affect people's lives'
- encourage pupils to investigate and 'develop what animates themselves and others'
- give pupils the opportunity to become emotionally and socially literate
- develop a compassionate culture within which all pupils feel valued, respecting themselves, each other and those who are different
- promote 'teaching styles which:
  ○ value pupils' questions and give them space for their own thoughts, ideas and concerns
  ○ enable pupils to make connections between aspects of their learning
  ○ encourage pupils to relate their learning to a wider frame of reference – for example, asking "why", "how" and "where" as well as "what"'
- be aware of and articulate the impact of spiritual development.

Let us end where we began – by stressing the integral link between spirituality and compassion by using language more eloquent, elevated and inspirational than has perhaps been used thus far in this chapter:

> I believe we are all capable of improvement. We can transform ourselves. If ... you were to spend a few minutes every day thinking about and trying to develop compassion, eventually compassion, the essence of spiritual practice, will become part of your life. When that happens I am convinced that not only will your life be happier but you will also make a direct contribution to peace and happiness in the world as a whole.
>
> (His Holiness the Dalai Lama,
> Foreword to Teasdale, 1999: xiv)

Chapter 4

Compassion through moral and social development

David Woods

Abstract

This chapter investigates the contribution of moral and social development to the overall ethos and culture of the compassionate school. Although these two aspects reinforce each other, they have been written about separately. Moral development is defined as the ability of pupils to make judgements about how to behave, understanding the reasons for such behaviour, reflecting upon rights, responsibilities and relationships. The way schools can deal with 'moral literacy', and a policy and programme on moral development, is explored through a range of suggested activities. In particular, detailed attention is paid to such aspects as character development, emotional intelligence, the rights-respecting school, behaviour policies and programmes and restorative justice highlighting some practical strategies.

Social development is defined as the development of social skills in different contexts, a willingness to participate in a number of social settings and an understanding of the way commission and societies function. Specific aspects of social development are explored, such as the citizenship curriculum, explicitly and implicitly, including the community dimension. Other experiences and enrichment activities are also examined, along with examples of primary and secondary pledges or guarantees. There is a detailed section on the student voice, with many practical suggestions and ideas for making the student voice heard.

Moral and social education are brought together at the end of the chapter under the heading of school ethos and culture, which is defined as a school's distinctive character, spirit and guiding beliefs. Shared values and a positive, common language are vital elements of a school culture – the glue that should hold everybody together and be a positive force for social and moral development with a compelling and inclusive moral purpose based on compassion, equity, social justice and unshakeable principles.

Introduction

In a society that is increasingly secular and multi-faith, schools need more than ever to promote a set of values to underpin moral and social development. As traditional institutions break down, schools are becoming the only institutions we can rely on to inculcate in young people the values and ethical underpinning on which our collective future depends. The research evidence is clear: schools that are values-driven have high expectations and demonstrate academic, professional and personal success. Although moral and social development reinforce each other, for the purpose of this chapter they are defined separately.

Moral development

There are several interpretations of what moral development means, but it is concerned with the ability of pupils to make judgements about how to behave and act, and their reasons for such behaviour, based on their understanding of rights, responsibilities and relationships. Ofsted's *School inspection handbook* for 2015 refers to three main aspects that demonstrate the moral development of pupils (para. 132):

- ability to recognize the difference between right and wrong, readily apply this understanding in their own lives and, in so doing, respect the civil and criminal law of England
- understanding of the consequences of their behaviour and actions
- interest in investigating and offering reasoned views about moral and ethical issues.

Other commentators refer to 'moral literacy' bringing together a range of activities and experiences to support moral development, such as assemblies, the personal, social, health and economic education (PSHE) programme, behaviour for learning, the citizenship curriculum and the student voice. A school's policy and programme on moral education will set out the school's agreed values and how they can be lived in practice, with particular reference to learning how to live together, social justice, character development and 'human flourishing' within the overall culture and ethos. We may sum this up in the term 'ethics' – which will be learned from the way the school operates, the way the staff and students interact, and the way the school interacts with the communities it serves. Culture and context vary, but there are values that are universal and vital, such as respecting opinions that are different from one's own, respecting individuals equally regardless of their race, gender, sexual orientation or origin, recognizing the diversity of life and accepting that society is more likely to be successful if the rule of law is in place. Ethical and moral development requires a good deal of self-understanding and self-discipline and, as we write, there is a renewed interest and debate over the role of character as part of moral development but also as one essential determinant of young people's life chances.

Character development

> Character is the psychological muscle that moral conduct requires.
>
> (Amitai Etzioni, cited in Goleman, 1996: 285)

Character development has always been part of the history of schooling. However, it now has particular relevance to ethics in moral philosophy and social science. The trend is towards promoting character development, as traditionally associated with private and residential schooling, particularly in disadvantaged areas. It is generally accepted that academic progress cannot be made unless it is accompanied by personal and social development. The KIPP public charter schools in the United States have made this a particular feature of their provision, including 'character report cards'. The ARK chain of schools in England do likewise, stressing the development of character as an essential part of academic success. Writing about international education, Michael Barber and colleagues (2012) stress the need for young people to develop character, resilience and leadership to be part of the school curriculum. They have devised a curriculum model and summarized what children should learn in a simple mathematical equation: Well educated = ethics (Knowledge + Thinking + Leadership). They argue that this combination is most likely to unleash in young people the qualities needed to be innovative in their work and life and constructive in their engagement with communities at every level from the local to the global.

At the University of Birmingham, the Jubilee Centre for Character and Virtues (2013) has produced a framework for character education in schools, upon which the compassionate taxonomy draws. They define character as 'a set of personal traits and dispositions that produce specific moral emotions, inform motivation and guide conduct. It is an umbrella term for all explicit and implicit education that helps young people develop personal strengths called virtues.'

They have developed a set of key principles (2013: 2):

- Character is largely caught through role-modelling and emotional contagion. School culture and ethos are therefore essential.
- Character should also be taught: direct teaching of character provides the rationale, language and tools to use in developing character elsewhere in and out of school.

- Character is the foundation for improved attainment, better behaviour and increased employability.
- Character should be developed in partnership with parents, employers and other community organisations.

The pamphlet goes on to explore the virtues that make up good character: civic character virtues required for engagement and responsible citizenship; moral character virtues that enable everybody to respond well in areas of experience such as compassion, self-discipline and justice; and performance character virtues, putting character habits into practice such as resilience, determination and creativity. It concludes that 'schools have a responsibility to cultivate the virtues, define and list those they want to prioritise and integrate them into all teaching and learning in and out of school' (4) and argue that 'character virtues should be reinforced everywhere: on the playing fields, in classrooms, corridors, interactions between teachers and students, in assemblies, posters, headteacher messages and communications, staff training and in relations with parents' (5).

The hallmark of character is self-discipline and self-control, or as Daniel Goleman has written, the development of emotional intelligence (1996). A related aspect of character is being able to motivate and guide oneself. Being able to put aside one's self-centred focus and impulse opens the way to empathy, to caring, altruism and compassion. Seeing things from another person's perspective breaks down biased stereotypes and so develops tolerance and the acceptance of differences, allowing people to live together in mutual respect. Goleman promotes the development of 'emotional literacy' through emotional self-awareness, managing emotions and harnessing emotions productively. This leads in turn to the better handling of relationships including sharing, cooperation, helpfulness, conflict resolution and better team-working. Many schools have developed their own emotional literacy programmes in the belief that if pupils feel good and can work cooperatively with others, they will learn better and flourish individually.

Schools have a central role in developing character through inculcating self-discipline, empathy and emotional intelligence and this enables commitment to moral values and compassionate education. It is not enough to instruct children about values: they have to practise them. Moral education becomes ingrained as experiences are repeated over and over again. In this sense, emotional literacy goes hand in hand with education for character, for moral development and for citizenship. Some schools have addressed this through a Social and Emotional Aspects of Learning programme (DfE, 2010a).

The rights-respecting school

In terms of moral development, some schools have not only explicitly defined their values but have developed the concept of the 'rights-respecting school', particularly with reference to UNICEF (1989) and the principles of the Convention on the Rights of the Child (CRC). This begins with the whole school community learning about the convention through house and school assemblies, displays and newsletters including parents and governors. It is embedded through charters and agreements based on the CRC, which helps everybody understand their responsibilities in relation to their rights, in the classroom and school. The language of CRC is modelled and students develop caring and empathy as well as their own well-being. Charters are on display in every classroom and in social spaces. The key elements of this approach are:

- whole-school policies are reviewed with reference to the CRC
- all operational plans at different levels incorporate the CRC values
- the school uses the CRC to inform and add value to its work within the school, local, UK and global communities
- the school consciously develops a rights-respecting ethos through assemblies, tutor time, displays, posters, charters and modelling language
- the students adhere to the standards agreed in their charters and all staff model rights-respecting language and behaviour
- students are empowered to be active citizens and learners through student leadership, creating safe and healthy environments, charity work, community work, sustainable development, international links and positive action to help others.

The school community provides a context for moral learning and experience in a number of ways. First, it brings together moral actions and the principles that underlie them. If pupils are to understand concepts such as fairness, justice and compassion, they must see those concepts exemplified by the adults with whom they deal. Second, it provides experiences that help to form and test moral convictions and to modify attitudes. The school serves as an arena in which pupils can come to terms with the fact that the views and feelings of others must be taken into account; that the interests of the institution must be weighed against those of individuals, and that the rational resolution of disagreement is possible and desirable.

Children should be able to feel that their school has a clear, consistent and secure moral framework that will help them explore the moral questions that affect them. Because so much moral education is carried on incidentally, there is a temptation to assume that school life and the normal programme of learning will produce a sufficiently broad range of experiences to prompt discussions and reflection. However, schools need to examine what they provide *intentionally* as well as that which arises *incidentally*, in order to ensure that children are given sufficient information and opportunities to use their initiative, to make informed choices, to exercise leadership and responsibility, to consider the consequences of their own actions and to develop positive moral qualities. There are many opportunities in the formal curriculum, using specific subjects and courses for children, to engage through informed discussion with issues that bear upon the individual and society. Schools should be able to map these, ensuring that they are embedded across the curriculum. If these are added to the informal curriculum, to relationships within the school community and the example of those in authority, and are supported by extra-curricular activities, this will make a powerful contribution both to moral and social education. In this sense:

> A school teaches in three ways:
> By what it teaches,
> By how it teaches,
> By the kind of place it is.
>
> (cited in Brighouse and Woods, 2006)

Behaviour

A school's behaviour policy and practices say a great deal about its approach to moral and social development overall. As a piece of paper, or a set of rules, the policy has little value. As a contribution to a shared ethos and to values, and to the strengthening of positive norms of behaviour and the reasons for them, it is of much greater value. It marks the point where rules overlap with norms, and shows that responsibility for sustaining these norms lies with every individual. The underlying philosophy around successful behaviour policies in schools is a shared understanding and responsibility for behaviour among everyone – staff and pupils alike – and an emphasis on pupils being able to co-manage the process. Good behaviour systems emphasize self-discipline and regulation, consistent practices and clearly defined routines.

The starting point is a recognition of the key principles embedded in effective moral and social education:

- All pupils are equal in value but they do not have equal starting points so the school must be responsive to pupils' disadvantage or needs and work for behaviour improving over time.

- The aim must always be for students to self-regulate their behaviour and become self-disciplined learners.
- Pupils construct their own behaviour but the school must help them manage it through teaching and discussion about the expected behaviour and recognize and reward pupils who do the right thing.
- All pupil behaviour has a consequence – positive or negative – but schools need to be fair and consistent in their responses.
- Pupils need to be dealt with in a consistent but not necessarily uniform manner, the least intrusive sanction being used to correct poor behaviour for individual pupils in the spirit of restorative justice.
- School should express their expectations in positive rather than negative terms, expecting pupils to rise to the challenge.

AN EXAMPLE OF A POSITIVE SET OF EXPECTATIONS:
- I am a resilient learner – I always try my best and learn to the best of my ability.
- I am a reflective learner – when someone is speaking I always listen and give my full attention.
- I am always in the right place at the right time doing the right thing.
- I respect others and avoid using words that may offend them.
- I am responsible for my learning and the learning of others.
- I am ready to learn and always have the right equipment for my lesson.
- I accept my responsibility in wanting to maintain good behaviour in the school.

These expectations are expressed positively, as attitudes and behaviour for learning, rather than a negative set of rules forbidding certain actions.

Once the principles and expectations are established in the school, pupils may receive certain rewards for particular behaviours. It is widely accepted that behaviour management requires multiple levels of action, one of which is punitive sanctions. However, Hattie and Yates comment that 'no major theory of learning recommends moving into positive modes in response to students' lack of co-operation ... the simple, thoroughly validated, proposition is that aversive control methods, such as criticism, shouting, sarcasm, belittlement or overt rudeness, are tactics that produce only a superficial level of student compliance' (2013).

Other behaviour experts argue that the guiding principle for behaviour management is a healthy balance between negative consequences for inappropriate behaviour and positive consequences for appropriate behaviour. The key word is 'balance' and the compassionate school always first considers a restorative justice approach, allowing the pupils to put right what they have done wrong and reflect on their actions, rather than immediate punishment. In some schools, teachers use visual aids, writing pupils' names on the board beneath happy and sad faces to show precisely the level that pupils have reached with regards to rewards and consequences. Larger schools log adherence to the behaviour system electronically. This allows staff to be systematic and proactive in their approach to pupils exhibiting poor behaviour and causing concern, giving them a chance to change their behaviour before they receive a consequence.

In a climate of compassion and restorative justice, the first consequence is often for pupils to stay behind at the end of the day, reflect on their behaviour and reconcile this with the teacher or other members of staff, although sanctions need to be in place for more serious incidents.

In a compassionate school, the emphasis is firmly on rewards rather than sanctions, and a good test for any school's behaviour policy is whether, this is really the case. Is explicit good behaviour rewarded, such as consistently excellent attendance and punctuality, positive contributions to lessons and contributions to the range of school activities? Rewards range from positive postcards home to merit badges, public acknowledgement, 'learner of the week' awards, with the emphasis on positive recognition and praise. Such a policy is reviewed through class discussion, pupil questionnaires and through the exercise of students' leadership with the ambition of building the capacity of others to be more self-regulating. The behaviour policy thus becomes a framework for moral and social development.

Restorative justice

Restorative approaches provide an underpinning ethos and philosophy for making and repairing relationships and for fostering a sense of social responsibility and shared accountability. There are many challenges in implementing a school-wide policy since the restorative approach may be at odds with deeply held notions about power, control and discipline. The focus is on responsibility and problem-solving, dialogue and negotiation; on repair, apology, reparation and interpersonal processes rather than blame or guilt, adversarial processes and punishment to deter. Where inappropriate and negative behaviour has caused harm, all sides need:

- a chance to tell their side of the story and feel heard
- to understand better how the situation happened
- to understand how it can be avoided another time
- to feel understood by the others involved
- to find a way to move on and feel better about themselves.

Restorative approaches are based on four key features, which are:

- respect – for everyone by listening to other opinions and learning to value them
- responsibility – taking responsibility for your own actions
- repair – developing skills within the school community to identify solutions that repair harm and ensure behaviours are not repeated
- re-integration – working through a structured, supportive process that aims to solve problems and allows children and young people to remain in mainstream education.

Restorative justice and peer mediation policies and programmes in schools use these key features as part of their approach. In both primary and secondary schools, peer mediators are trained and deployed to discuss disagreements and issues calmly and rationally, moving towards a solution with conferences convened by members of staff between the perpetrator, the victim and the peer mediator. Staff are also trained to make this a whole-school approach.

The compassionate school seeks to deal with conflict in a way that meets everybody's needs so that those involved can repair the damage done. Because they have been listened to, pupils in conflict are now ready to listen to others' perspectives and so empathy is developed. Punitive disciplinary responses, on the other hand, can cause resentment rather than reflection, do not repair relationships, can lead to further alienation and are often not considered fair. Schools that have had the most success in the implementation of restorative approaches are those that see these as part of the general development of relationship skills, emotional literacy, collaborative teaching and learning, and peer support. They seek to build cohesive, compassionate communities underpinned by their values and ethos.

Social development

In contrast to moral development, it might be felt that social development is much less problematic although, clearly, limited social mobility, income inequality and immediate social context do present a variety of challenges to individual schools.

According to Ofsted, pupils' social development is shown by:

- use of a wide range of social skills in different contexts, including working and socializing with pupils from different religions, ethics and socioeconomic backgrounds

- willingness to participate in a variety of social settings, including volunteering, cooperating well with others, and being able to resolve conflicts effectively
- interest in, and understanding of, the way communities and societies function at a variety of levels.

This recognizes two closely interwoven strands in pupils' personal development: personal relationships and the entitlement to learn in an environment in which there are good standards of behaviour marked by respect and responsibility; and the school's curriculum and the way it is taught to children and received by them.

We can say that pupils demonstrate effective social development if, at a level appropriate to their age and ability, they display:

- the ability to make a strong contribution to the well-being of social groups and to form effective relationships with them
- the skills involved in taking on the roles of leaders and team-workers exercising responsibility, initiative and cooperation, often expressed through the student voice
- attitudes that show the capacity to adjust to a range of social contexts through appropriate behaviour
- understanding of the ways in which societies function and are organized (family, school, local, national and international), which can be taught explicitly through a citizenship curriculum
- understanding of how individuals relate to each other and to the institutions, structures and processes of society as a whole.

The citizenship curriculum

In the ongoing debate about the place of social and moral education in the curriculum and whether this is explicit or implicit, many schools have chosen to teach citizenship explicitly in the sense that this is timetabled in certain years of the primary and secondary curriculum. Staff in schools are aware of the students' need both for social engagement and active citizenship and also for learning particular knowledge and understanding. Clearly, instruction will only be effective if it can be integrated with young people's emerging understanding and experience of themselves and the communities they inhabit. The most obvious of these communities is the school. It is the starting point for developing active, democratic citizenship through an exploration of what values, principles, rights and duties mean in practice. Schools could arguably be seen as city states in their own right, with their own interests, rights and responsibilities, where pupils begin to develop their social and community skills. Opportunities for debate, reflection and shared decision-making can be utilized from the earliest age to have a positive impact upon motivation, responsibility and behaviour. These opportunities should include cooperation, participation and conflict resolution so that the framework of learning to be a citizen and a moral and social being begins in the family and the school.

The next stage is to enable young people to develop into active, responsible citizens – first with the local communities that young people encounter every day, then with the nation state and then as 'global' citizens. This demands knowledge, understanding and skills. First, schools need to be able to explain and articulate their agenda for citizenship, defining a common core of knowledge, concepts and understanding central to being a citizen. Second, pupils need opportunities to develop their understanding of social rules and principles. These can be taught through dedicated learning time, perhaps as part of PSHE education, through specific citizenship lessons or from relevant aspects of National Curriculum subjects. Opportunities for reflection and discussion need to be maximized using appropriate techniques and resources. This kind of discussion and development strengthens the potential for pupils to take responsibility for themselves and those around them, using their social skills in different contexts. They also include trusting students with responsibility for peer education and feedback: opportunities to hear from people beyond the school – governors, employers, religious leaders, community leaders and councillors, discussing matters of interest and concern with them – play an important part in this process.

Fostering community cohesion has long been a priority for schools and a range of community organizations and agencies, despite income inequality and little social mobility, and this remains a legally established priority for schools. Community cohesion means different things for different schools, often depending upon a notion of place – from the complexities of the inner city to a remote, rural area. Broadly speaking, the school can define its communities as the people who live, work and associate in close proximity. The term 'community' can be understood in terms of cultural, religious or ethnic groups.

While the individual school will in almost all cases reflect community cohesion, this is not necessarily the case for the surrounding communities, who may be contributing to a problematic learning environment regarding social and moral education. For example, there may be a crossover of negative characteristics from the local community reflecting social and racial disharmony and even open conflict, particularly in complex, urban schools. This can make community engagement extremely problematic.

Indeed, certain schools have sought to ensure that their values are not unduly influenced by an outside community disadvantaging their pupils and isolating them from opportunity. Such schools seek to reach beyond their immediate communities, instructing their students that 'the street stops at the gate', although careful to demonstrate the positive aspects of school-community engagement and to make themselves a hub for a range of learning, social opportunities. Perhaps the major part of the citizenship agenda is to understand the way societies function at a variety of levels including that of the nation and the world. Young people now have immediate access to news and information and more than ever need to understand the institutions, structures and processes that govern their country and the world.

Whatever the community dimension, it is important that schools encourage their pupils to work towards a society that has a sense of belonging for all communities: a society in which the diversity of people's backgrounds and circumstances is appreciated and valued; a society in which opportunities are available to all and in which strong and positive relationships continue to be developed in schools and community. There should be opportunities for pupils to learn from other people, places and organizations so that they can engage with a range of experiences that challenge their thinking. Some schools have established volunteering programmes to work on community projects.

Experiences, enrichment and entitlements

An important aspect of the school curriculum is how it relates to life in society, taking advantage of student curriculum time and extra-curricular activities to keep the school together as a community and assume greater responsibility for their actions in and beyond school, as well as taking pride in their achievements. There is a strong case for a school formally agreeing and then publishing to the local community a 'guaranteed' set of experiences that all pupils should enjoy and then, with their governors, involving the various agencies locally and the pupils' parents in making sure that all the pupils have such experiences as an entitlement. The extra money allocated via the Pupil Premium can help fund these experiences for disadvantaged pupils. Of course, debate on what these experiences should be may reveal a mismatch between what heads and staff would provide in their own families, and the perceptions of the local community. But we know that many schools have managed, through consultation, to come up with an agreed set of experiences. In the 1990s, Birmingham local authority led the way for all its schools by producing guidance on a set of guarantees for early years, primary and secondary schools, which could be implemented by schools. The London Challenge (n.d.) produced a similar 'pupil pledge' as an example for London schools to follow. Where this is adapted by schools in the primary phase, there is usually a focus on experiences that all those working in and with schools, including parents and community groups, would help to provide.

AN EXAMPLE OF A PRIMARY SCHOOL PLEDGE OR GUARANTEE
The school would guarantee that pupils would:

- take part in a public performance at least twice during their primary years
- take part in supporting charities and community projects during their primary years
- by the age of seven, have had an opportunity to have extra coaching in some aspect of the expressive arts that they have appeared to have an interest in or passion for, linked to outside agencies
- be in a group creating a book or multimedia DVD, which would be suitable for another age group, present it and then collectively critique it
- take part in a residential experience during Key Stage 2
- in Year 6, take part in an environmental study relevant to their local community.

AN EXAMPLE OF A SECONDARY SCHOOL PLEDGE OR GUARANTEE
The school would guarantee that pupils would:

- take part in voluntary programmes through a range of community projects during their secondary years
- by the age of 12, have had the opportunity to take part in a literary performance
- by the age of 13, have been involved in an activity that utilizes ICT skills and is demonstrable to parents
- by the age of 14, have had the opportunity to be involved in an artistic performance or physical activity involving the community
- by the age of 15, have had the opportunity to celebrate languages by using their knowledge of community, European and world languages to support the activities of others
- by the age of 16, have had participated in a quality work experience placement as part of a planned programme of work-related activities
- by the age of 18, have had the opportunity for an out-of-school challenge linked to the community and involving self-organization.

The student voice

The student voice is a vital ingredient of the social dimension of schooling and features strongly in debates about the 'co-construction' of school experiences where the co-constructors are the pupils. That is to say, they are partners with staff in planning, devising and delivering the outcomes. However, schools vary considerably in their attention to this aspect of schooling.

School councils are often as far as this gets, and their influence on school life can be marginal if participants are drawn from a narrow range of students: the more able and more fluent. Some schools, however, have involved pupils not just in specific leadership initiatives but in influencing departments and faculties, engaging in leading learning and having a real say in every aspect of school life.

In some secondary schools, the school council is elevated to, and recognized as, a fundamental part of student voice: it is even called 'student voice' and instantly takes on a whole-school dimension. Opportunity is provided in the same schools, during tutor time, for all students – along with their tutor as part of the group – to voice their concerns and raise issues for the council to consider. These sessions are led by the council representatives, who raise issues for the next council meeting to consider. The meeting is timetabled and held within two weeks of the session. The representatives report back to the tutor group two weeks later on the outcome and further discussion takes place. This happens each half term. This managed, student-centred approach to school council, with student voice at its heart, gives the whole process democratic credibility, with student ownership and direct input into school improvement. All students are encouraged to take part and everyone's opinion is judged to be valid and valued. This, in turn, contributes to raising pupils' self-confidence and esteem, enhancing responsible and respectful communication, and acknowledgement that students' views matter and that taking part can make a difference.

This is easier at primary level where primary teachers involve the pupils in the daily management of the classroom, allocating pupil monitors who have applied for different tasks and then carry out their regular jobs. It's surprising that, on transfer to secondary schools, this practice stops – just when, in Year 7, most pupils would wish for ways to impress.

Recognizing that pupils need a voice, most primary, special and secondary schools have a school council. Without careful planning, however, this can soon become an irrelevance. It must have consequences for the whole school community so requires:

- a budget with strings attached, that is, it needs to affect the whole school environment
- task groups, to which other pupils need to be co-opted and charged with investigating various real issues in the school, for example attendance, homework, marking practices, extra-curricular activities, school rules and sanctions, use of student surveys, induction and 'buddying' arrangements for new arrivals, school communication policies and practices
- codes of operation – minutes, chairing, progress-chasing prior to meeting.

In large secondary schools, school councils nowadays often need to be related to year councils and/or houses or colleges or the emerging 'schools-within-schools', often with vertical tutor groups. Whatever the state of a school council, students should legitimately be involved in most of the school's activities, but certainly:

- in the overall design and planning of the spiritual, moral, social and cultural (SMSC) provision
- within the classroom – in managing roles and in self-assessment as part of assessment for learning
- as peer tutors – an excellent way of learning and modifying behaviour for older pupils who are tasked to help younger ones (interestingly, the Sutton Trust and Education Endowment Foundation (2013) found that peer interventions are among the three that have the most impact on school outcomes)
- as peer mentors – within and beyond the classroom or tutor group
- as peer counsellors and mediators – to aid behaviour in and around school and act as a guard against bullying (some schools have pupil juries to deal with bullying and other disciplinary issues)
- as 'community workers' – helping locally as part of citizenship programmes
- as editors and contributors to a magazine produced by pupils
- in interpreting and reporting back on the annual review – through pupil surveys of school ethos and pupils' commitment to the life of the school and their willingness to learn, such reports being fed to the senior leadership team and governors
- as observer members of the governing body and its sub-committees
- as part of the appointment process for new staff – including the headteacher.

12 ideas for making the students' voice heard

1. Make sure you use pupils to buddy any new pupil: two each is much better than one.

2. Try making an expectation that all sixth formers spend at least a specified time in lessons lower down the school, and also in primary schools in, for example, their after school clubs. Incorporate their work into their reports.

3. Make pupil presentations a planned part of lessons and establish a rota whereby pupils take turns to lead parts of lessons.

4. Let pupils introduce all new topics: they are told what it will be and given free rein to present it however they like. Teachers feed back on how they have done and there is a term prize for the best.

5. Make sure class captains have jobs to do.

6. Let students with 'expert' knowledge teach the class.

7. Train a group of pupils to review teaching and learning in the school.

8. Seek pupil feedback on what went well and what could be improved in lessons – 'even better ifs' (EBIs).

9. Each year group trains up groups of pupils to take charge of displays, and allows the pupils to set up new displays.

10. Have pupils in rotation on reception and feed back on their performance in reports.

11. Involve students in twos and threes as co-mentors and coaches so they try to solve issues about learning before going to the teacher.

12. Allow pupils to 'self-elect' into a series of teams, which have a clear purpose, such as 'the green team', leading on environmental issues; 'we love art and design team', improving experiences in the school; or the 'literacy team', encouraging pupils to read.

School ethos and culture

Social and moral education in particular contribute significantly to the culture and ethos of a school – its distinctive character, spirit and guiding beliefs. This has a powerful effect on the quality of relationships and the effectiveness of teaching and learning and is paramount in obtaining a successful learning environment. It is composed of many ingredients, including: high expectations, character development, compassion, citizenship, personalized support, pride in achievement and getting the best from everyone. An ethos that is conducive to high morale and high expectations in the whole school community is not a matter of accident but a product of good leadership at every level. School leaders have a crucial role in communicating, developing and applying the vision and values of the school. This is expressed through the ways in which members of a school community relate to each other and work together, the sense of shared purpose and mutual commitment. It is not easy to talk about values, as they need to be practised on an experiential level rather than at a cognitive level so that ethos goes hand in hand with education for moral and social development.

> School leadership is a profoundly moral, ethical and emotional activity designed to encourage a school's staff to build and act on a shared and evolving vision of enhanced educational experiences for pupils.
>
> (Stoll *et al.*, 2003)

A school's values will inform the whole community's actions, particularly the values of those who lead and have the most influence upon the school community, namely the headteacher, staff and pupils with a leadership role. They have to live with the knowledge that there has to be a consistent thread between what they say, what they do, and who they are. This brings us to the crucial importance of the type of language used, which can either make or break a school. If the wrong language is used in assemblies, tutor groups, lessons or in everyday contact, it can sap the energy and motivation of the school community. On the other hand, the right language can encourage, stimulate and energize everybody. In lessons and elsewhere, for example, using 'we' rather than 'I' and 'you' is important when working and learning together for success. In terms of the compassionate school, the use of a common language is worth keeping under review, checking its application and impact from time to time.

> One of the simplest and at the same time most important ways in which we signal the degree of empathetic engagement is through the language we use.
>
> (Lucas, 2009: 204)

In terms of school culture, we know that every school will claim to have explicit values and beliefs but the test is how far this is shared by the whole school community. Culture is the glue that should hold everybody together and be a positive force for moral and social development. It manifests itself in customs, symbols, stories, language and norms of behaviour. Where a school has a positive culture, there is a compelling and inclusive moral purpose throughout the school, based on equity, compassion, social justice and unshakeable principles linked closely to the 'acts for love', the taxonomy of compassion expanded in this book's first chapter. In such schools, we would expect to see and experience shared values among all the members of the community: transparency and openness, generosity of spirit, and mutual respect. Compassion through moral and social development will be generated through a positive school curriculum and culture, through community engagement at all levels, an understanding of moral and ethical issues, and a willingness to participate in a variety of social contexts.

So, although the agenda for school is large, you might want to adopt the following manageable strategies:

- become a 'rights-respecting school' working with UNICEF on implementing the Convention on the Rights of the Child
- develop a policy and programme for restorative justice
- develop a student pledge for your school
- extend the student voice using some or all of the 12 ideas
- construct an explicit DNA for your school ethos, culture and compassion.

Chapter 5

Compassion through cultural development

Gilroy Brown and Maurice Irfan Coles

*My own eyes are not enough for me, I will see through those of
others. Reality, even seen through the eyes of many, is not enough.
I will see what others have invented ... . In reading great literature
I become a thousand men and yet remain myself. Like the night
sky in the Greek poem, I see with myriad eyes, but it is still I who
see. Here, as in worship, in love, in moral action, and in knowing,
I transcend myself; and am never more myself than when I do.*
(C.S. Lewis, *An Experiment in Criticism*, 1961)

Abstract

All education systems transmit their own view of culture and cultural
development, whether or not they are part of their stated aims. Since 1988
the duty to promote the cultural development of pupils and society has been
a statutory requirement in England and is Ofsted-inspected. Although many
of this chapter's examples are drawn from this context (and much of it from
the work over time of Coles and his associates), the underlying principles
have universal significance. Definitions of culture are not and have never been
neutral, but reflect the contemporary dominant values of society. This chapter
unpicks the creative and anthropological perspectives on culture and relates
them to their transmission and development within schools. It explores the
dynamic and interactive relationship between culture and identity, and argues
that, especially when viewed through the prism of compassion, cultural
development is a key vehicle for helping young people become skilled and
compassionate cultural navigators in an age of multiple identities.

Introduction

On the face of it, there is a seeming paradox between compassionate
education – which aims to foster selfless love and to remove the 'I' from
identity – and an education system that encourages high self-esteem and
personal advancement. The paradox is, however, more apparent than real
for a secure sense of self, of being at ease within one's own skin and identity,

and within one's culture, is a necessary prerequisite for high attainment and for a better understanding and appreciation of the 'other'. Well over half a century ago, Eric Fromm (1957) recognized that if young people were self-aware, if they manifested self-love, not in a narcissistic arrogant way but in a way that allowed them to take responsibility for their actions, then they would be more compassionate, more open to other cultures.

The terms culture and cultural development are, however, not neutral, but are contested for they go to the very heart of what we teach, and our vision of the type of society we wish to create. Latterly, heated political and educational debates have raged around terms like multicultural and intercultural. To begin to understand these complexities and their implications for the development of compassionate schooling, we require clarity of definition and realistic translation into classroom and whole-system practice. There are two distinct but interrelated perspectives on culture – the creative and the anthropological – which come together in the pupil's experience and which have considerable impact, especially if approached through the prism of compassion. The first, *the creative*, concerns itself with the creation of, participation in and enjoyment of a range of artistic, sporting, scientific and mathematical activities, which on the face of it may not appear to be contentious. In schools, however, issues relate to the amount of time spent on such activities, and the nature of creative provision, especially when compared with the core dominant academic subjects of English, maths and science (all of which can be taught creatively). All education systems transmit their view of culture and cultural development, whether or not they appear as part of their explicit aims.

The second, *the anthropological*, relates to the beliefs, values, customs and sense of meaning shared by a particular group and, in the case of education, how those shared values are transmitted. This refers to the curriculum offer: what we teach, what we choose not to teach, and the perspectives we bring.

Being culturally developed is not the same as simply enjoying the Arts, in the sense of relishing that which we traditionally describe as 'high culture'. Far from it: Hitler would weep at Wagner and his coterie adored (and stole) Europe's finest paintings, yet their ability to empathize in the context of the Arts was clearly totally disconnected from any compassion for humanity. By contrast, being culturally developed requires a range of creative skills and attitudes, knowledge and understanding that encourage openness, empathy and appreciation of national and international cultural traditions; and a willingness to challenge all forms of prejudice, discrimination and injustice – key characteristics that are the bedrock of a compassionate person.

Culture: The creative perspective

Commonly, culture is seen as either 'popular' or 'high', with value judgements often made as to which is the better. High culture is associated with being educated, with being 'cultured', with appreciating and possibly creating the finer things in life. This creative perspective is easily understood through the words of the eminent Victorian educationalist and poet Mathew Arnold, as 'the best that has been thought and said'; we might add, 'and done'. Sometimes used to justify a narrow more nationalistic curriculum, Arnold was, in fact, far more global in his vision:

> The whole scope of the essay is to recommend culture as the great help out of our present difficulties; culture being a pursuit of our total perfection by means of getting to know, on all the matters which most concern us, *the best which has been thought and said in the world*, and, through this knowledge, turning a stream of fresh and free thought upon our stock notions and habit.
>
> (Arnold, 1869, Preface: 4)

Arnold's notion of the best has been widely used; but his creative 'turning a stream of fresh and free thought' often ignored. Always disputed, it goes to the heart of the educational philosophy, which juxtaposes the learning of content against the firing of the imagination. Even in Arnold's own era, this was a contested space, wonderfully satirized by Charles Dickens in *Hard Times* (1854) in the person of Thomas Gradgrind, a headteacher who famously argued that children should be taught 'facts, facts, facts'. The transmission of facts predominate in the latest version of the English National Curriculum (DfE, 2014b), which is based upon Hirsch's concept of 'cultural literacy', which maintains that 'creativity depends on mastering skills and acquiring a body of knowledge before being able to give expression to what's in you' (cited in RSA, 2014: 33).

English politicians responsible for the curriculum remained robustly deaf to the chorus of professional expert disapproval of statutory curriculum changes, contemptuously dismissing those who, like Professor Ken Robinson, had argued for a balanced curriculum that supported both teaching creatively *and* the teaching of creativity. Robinson chaired the National Advisory Committee on Creative and Cultural Education (NACCCE), which in 1999 published the seminal *All Our Futures*, arguing that creativity was a basic capacity of human intelligence that was possible in all areas of activity. All children, Committee members believed, have creative abilities that, with effective teaching, could be realized for the personal and common good. Teaching for creativity aimed to encourage autonomy, authenticity, openness, respect and personal fulfilment – characteristics remarkably similar to those of the compassionate person. In his later writings and his internationally famous TED talks, Robinson went on to champion what he called the 'Element', the place where the aptitude of the individual meets his or her personal passion. As he described it, 'to be in your Element is more than doing things you are good at ... to be in your Element you have to love it, too' (Robinson and Aronica, 2013: xii). One of the major functions of education is to help young people to find, then nurture, their creative element.

For Robinson, contemporary education is blighted by the dominance of the Programme for International Student Assessment (PISA) tables, where the measuring of a narrow range of academic subjects distorts and disables wider educational provision and 'squeezes out' creativity (Robinson, 2014). Creativity, like compassion, is not easily subject to assessment regimes and cannot simply be sound-bitten for league table purposes. In part as a response to this dilemma, the Centre for Real-World Learning based at the University of Winchester, in their *Progression in Creativity: Developing new forms of assessment* (Spencer *et al.*, 2012: 34–5), pioneered the Five Creative Dispositions Model in which they outlined five creative learning habits, which could be used as a possible assessment tool as well as a workable definition of the creative.

Table 5.1: Creative learning habits and sub-habits of mind

Habit of mind	*Sub-habits of mind*
1. Inquisitive	Wondering and questioning
	Exploring and investigating
	Challenging assumptions
2. Persistent	Tolerating uncertainty
	Sticking with difficulty
	Daring to be different
3. Imaginative	Playing with possibilities
	Making connections
	Using intuition
4. Disciplined	Crafting and improving
	Developing techniques
	Reflecting critically
5. Collaborative	Cooperating appropriately
	Giving and receiving feedback
	Sharing the 'product'

Coles and Scoble (2012) effectively used these habits as key development tools in their Sacred Spaces Project: Developing a Creative and Cultural Curriculum in Faith-Based Settings, in which they placed artists in four faith-based supplementary schools in London and Leicester. After working with different artistic forms to explore their concept of the sacred, the young participants collaboratively shared their work and insights in a celebratory event held at the Royal Society in London. One parent movingly described the pupil interaction as 'like the United Nations in action with young people of different cultures and faiths coming together in a shared enterprise'. For the young people involved, the experience was significant not merely because they had acquired new skills but also new attitudes. As one participant put it in his evaluation interview, 'One thing I will do differently as a result of being involved in this project is that I would respect different religions more because I know more about them' (Coles and Scoble, 2012: 8).

The Sacred Spaces Project provided a clear example of NACCCE's earlier assertion that 'the engine for cultural change is the human coactivity for creative thought and action' (1999: 6). Creative processes, however, do not exist in vacuums but are contextually bound and draw ideas from the cultural milieus in which they take place. In order to develop, young people need an understanding of these contexts. A starting point is to recognize and validate the cultural expertise and experiences of all groups, including minority ethnic groups. To understand other cultures and ways of seeing, we need to engage with their music, visual art, verbal and performing arts; to appreciate something of their religious and historical backgrounds, so that, like C.S. Lewis, they might see through the eyes of others, to see with myriad eyes; in short, to begin to understand something of cultural anthropology.

Culture: The anthropological perspective

The visionary 1944 English Education Act referred to pupils' moral, spiritual, physical and mental development; but not to their cultural. Forty-four years later, the 1988 Education Reform Act incorporated cultural development as a statutory requirement for all state-maintained schools, presumably because the Britain of 1944 bore little resemblance to the Britain of 1988, which, by then, had become a place of many cultures and of great diversity. England, like Canada, the United States, Australia and elsewhere, is now a country of super/hyper-diversity, with populations that include an enormous array of cultures, heritages, languages, faiths and ethnicities. The implications for our education services are profound, as teachers have to provide a curriculum, pedagogy and a set of values that help all children both to achieve and to live together harmoniously in these mega-multicultural global societies.

In retrospect, some English local education authorities (LEAs), like the Royal Borough of Berkshire and the Inner London Education Authority (ILEA), were amazingly prescient in attempting to prepare their pupils for life in multicultural societies. City of Birmingham Education Department, for example, as long ago as 1985, published its seminal document, *Education for Our Multicultural Society*, with its twin drivers of cultural diversity and anti-racism and which, in part, helped to shape the thinking of many other local and national bodies. Indeed, it still provides one of the shortest, simplest and most practical explications of some of the key contemporary multicultural issues.

The authors of *Education for Our Multicultural Society* based their detailed report on Birmingham's succinct 1981 policy statement, which exhorted schools to combat racism, to build on the strengths of cultural diversity and 'to provide for the particular needs of pupils having regard for their racial ethnic, cultural, historical, linguistic and religious backgrounds' (City of Birmingham Education Department, 1985: 5). The report stressed the teaching of the values of our multicultural democracy; and argued that it was 'important that all pupils learn to understand the forces making for cohesion, as well as the factors which may cause tension and disharmony' (31). In addition, they urged schools to help pupils to recognize their own place and role in the management of conflict and the maintenance of peaceful collaboration between all members of society. The dominant concept of culture was defined as 'the child's total lived experience', which, the authors maintained, was dynamic and evolving, and counselled schools against any approach that reduced culture to the exotic, to what the late Barry Troyna called the 3 Ss of 'saris, steel bands and samosas'.

'The child's total lived experience', however, like all experience, is only understood through the lens of our identity. The same event can be interpreted differently according to our perception, and our belief about ourselves, which in part is determined by our feeling of belonging, of being a member of a group that fosters and nurtures us and that has its own cultural norms. The original Latin word *cultura* meant 'cultivation' and was first coined by Cicero, who wrote of *cultura animi*, 'the cultivation of the soul'. Transposed to education, it re-appeared in modern Europe in the seventeenth century referring to the betterment or refinement of individuals. Later, it was applied to whole peoples, and discussion of the term was often connected to national aspirations or ideals; and, as in the case of Britain in the twenty-first century, it generated a very lively and ongoing debate about national identity in an increasingly pluralistic setting.

Identity derives from the Latin *idem*, meaning 'the same', and relates both to the concepts and characteristics that belong to you as an individual – your sense of self-image, self-esteem and self-reflection – and the characteristics shared by members of your group. The key question for educators is what constitutes these characteristics, and how they relate to the curriculum and classroom pedagogy. Following the horrific 7/7 London bombings in 2005, Coles was commissioned to undertake a series of in-service sessions in various parts of England related to extremism and radicalization. Discussion about the nature of extremism was always preceded by work on the forces perceived by the participants to have fashioned their own identities. The respondents consistently listed the things in Figure 5.1 as key determining forces that made up their identities.

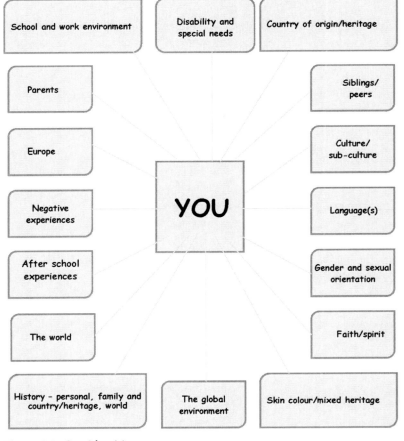

Figure 5.1: Our identities

What became clear was that our sense of self is contained within our notion of identity, an identity which for young people is shaped by the totality of their experiences – at home, in the street, playground and school, on social media and in the wider world. We, like them, live in an age of multiple overlapping identities, which alter at different times and in different contexts so that the type of language and behaviours we use in a professional context, for example, is likely to be different from those we use with our peers in social contexts; and different again from our interactions with our own parents. One major, and possibly age-related, omission from the professionals' lists, however, was technology or more precisely hyper-connectivity. A fascinating British government report, *Future Identities: Changing identities in the UK – the next 10 years*, explores this in some depth (Foresight, 2013).

The report argues that 'the emergence of hyper-connectivity (where people can now be constantly connected online), the spread of social media, and the increase in online personal information, are key factors which will interact to influence identities' (1). They set these developments within the wider context of demographic change in a Britain that is ever more plural, and where more social interaction between diverse groups will increasingly occur. For them, 'the UK is now a virtual environment as well as a real place, and increasingly UK citizens are globally networked individuals. Hyper-connectivity not only has the potential to increase the pace of social change, but may also make it more volatile. As such, the internet has not produced a new kind of identity. Rather, it has been instrumental in raising awareness that identities are more multiple, culturally contingent and contextual than had previously been understood' (1).

For schools, understanding and responding to these culturally contingent and contextual factors is the hallmark of cultural development. Since 1988, definitions of cultural development have undergone continuous refinement by British government agencies. That provided by Ofsted (2004), although revised in 2014 to include a non-statutory duty for schools to promote British values, essentially captures it:

> Cultural development is about pupils understanding their own culture and other cultures in their town, region and in the country as a whole. It is about understanding cultures represented in Europe and elsewhere in the world. It is about understanding and feeling comfortable in a variety of cultures and being able to operate in the emerging world culture of shared experiences provided by television, travel and the internet. It is about understanding that cultures are always changing and coping with change. Promoting

pupils' cultural development is intimately linked with schools' attempts to value cultural diversity and prevent racism' (Ofsted, 2004: 23).

'Their own and other cultures' includes an understanding and appreciation of their linguistic, religious, ethnic, historical, and 'racial' characteristics, especially as they relate to the needs of pupils and of society; and to approaches that help young people be empathetic to their own and other cultures. Pupils do not start school as blank sheets eagerly waiting for teachers to impose their own scripts. They come with a wealth of cultural capital from home and society, upon which schools can build.

The UK, for example, is home to over 600 living languages and many young children start school with a linguistic fluency in one, and sometimes two or even three community/heritage languages. Our system, with its historical antipathy to learning languages other than English, still fails to capitalize effectively on this cultural capital, in spite of overwhelming evidence that second language learning can not only aid the acquisition of English, but also help to build personal esteem and wider understanding. As Dame Helen Wallace of the British Academy put it in *The Guardian*'s *Loving Languages* special report (*Guardian*, 2014), 'there are cognitive and personal benefits to supporting community languages and the languages are important for keeping the cultural connections of those with a shared heritage'. In the same article, Daniel Kaufman, executive director of the Endangered Language Alliance, similarly argued that 'encouraging heritage languages leads to a multilingual society that is better equipped to communicate with the world ... Just as importantly, it can help prevent children from being alienated from their own home culture; this by itself, has important psychological consequences for the individual, communities and ultimately the larger society in question.'

Further alienation is also likely if schools do not take account of the historical backgrounds, cultural heritages and perspectives of plural populations. UNESCO categorizes these heritages as tangible, intangible and natural. *Tangible* includes movables, such as paintings, sculptures, coins and manuscripts, and immovables, such as monuments and archaeological artefacts. *Intangible* relates to oral traditions, performing arts and rituals; and *natural* includes sites such as cultural landscapes and physical, biological or geological formations. British schools have come a long way in incorporating wide examples of cultural heritages and perspectives since the earlier more Anglocentric interpretations and concentrations. For example, many utilize the significant expertise and resources of Black History Month (www.blackhistorymonth.org.uk), of Facing History and Ourselves (www. facinghistory.org) and the amazing work of the 1001 Inventions organization, exploring Muslim heritage in our world (*www.1001inventions.com*).

Prior to the recent changes, all English National Curriculum subjects were required to explore international aspects of cultural, ethnic and religious diversity and 'how these have shaped the world' (QCA, 2007: 112). But in history, for example, this breadth was replaced by a narrower curriculum that requires students to 'know and understand the history of these islands as a coherent, chronological narrative, from the earliest times to the present day: how people's lives have shaped this nation and how Britain has influenced and been influenced by the wider world' (DfE, 2014b: 232) – a very different take on the purpose of teaching history.

These recent changes were loudly decried by the teaching profession and historical associations; but even greater wrath was reserved for the calculated destruction of many of the hard-won structures and systems that were in place to support race equality in schools. Chris Keats, leader of one of the largest teaching unions, in a speech at the British Schools and the Black Child conference (2014), provided a snapshot of the government's education reforms, which she considered to be 'a backward step in race equality in schools, not only for black and minority ethnic children and young people but also for black and minority ethnic teachers' (Brown and Coles, 2014: 31). She listed six areas of significant negative change even without reference to curriculum.

At the same conference, black educator and former headteacher, Rosemary Campbell-Stephens, in an impassioned speech attacking the Coalition government's implicit policy of de-racializing education, warned people not to delude themselves that they are living in a post-racial age: 'I feel that white supremacy every day,' she said. She singled out the UK's history curriculum for particular criticism, 'reducing us to slaves ... I want a UK history that tells the truth that the real reason for the First World War was the fight over re-dividing Africa ... and that the foundations of the industrial revolution were built on enslaving the African people'(Brown and Coles, 2014: 32).

Worryingly, research published in 2014 by the British Social Attitudes Survey (NatCen, 2014) found that nearly a third of people in the UK admitted to being racially prejudiced, and that the proportion had increased since the start of the century, returning us to levels seen 30 years ago. We no longer suffer from theories of crude eugenics, or the causal acceptance of racist behaviours in the workplace and on the street; and most people now recognize the social not biological construction of 'race'. But attitudes in parts of the UK seem resistant to change and, even more worryingly, institutional racism appears stubbornly difficult to shift. There is still considerable evidence of institutional racism clearly defined in the Macpherson report (1999: 6.34) as 'the collective failure of an organization to provide an appropriate and professional service to people because of their colour, culture, or ethnic origin ... which ... can be seen or detected in processes, attitudes and behaviour which amount to discrimination through unwitting prejudice, ignorance, thoughtlessness and racist stereotyping which disadvantage minority ethnic people'. David Gillborn, in his *Racism and Education: Coincidence or Conspiracy?* (2008), goes further, utilizing critical race theory to present a detailed and damning indictment of education policy, which he controversially argues is not designed to eliminate race inequality but to sustain it at manageable levels.

Education 'reforms' reinforced the onslaught on multicultural paradigms by Prime Minister David Cameron, when he argued in a speech in Munich in 2011 that what he called state multiculturalism had failed. As Cameron put it, 'under the doctrine of state multiculturalism, we have encouraged different cultures to live separate lives, apart from each other and the mainstream' (Cameron, 2011). Analysis of the speech sheds no light on the evidential genesis of this opinion. It further reveals that Cameron (like Tony Blair before him) was essentially concerned about Muslims, the war on terror and the extreme views of a very small minority of adherents.

For schools, however, the issues go to the heart of how they respond to the religious needs of their Muslim pupils; what is acceptable accommodation and how they approach Muslim issues with non-Muslim pupils. Sharing of faith backgrounds and interfaith interactions have always been viewed as one of the strengths of an English education system that encouraged the teaching of religious education. But the treatment of large concentrations of Muslims in secular state schools has proved more problematic. The so-called 'Trojan Horse' affair in 2014, the central government response to a hoax letter relating to Muslim 'takeovers' in some Birmingham schools, brought this issue into sharper and even more contested focus. The conflation of race and religion into what has been termed 'anti-Muslim racism' and the spreading of 'moral panic' had already been clearly articulated by Insted (2014), whose website contains a range of materials offering an alternative narrative to the dominant British government discourse.

The response to the hoax, the dubious use of the Ofsted inspection process, two contested reports and the government's decision to require schools to actively promote 'fundamental British values' (as if, mysteriously, they were not already doing so) have added fuel to an already volatile situation. Richardson and Bolloten (2014) offer a searing critique of the

British government's present confused and confusing position. As a result, only three things appear certain: the articulated outrage of many citizens (and not just Muslims), the negative impact upon the identity of British Muslim students, and the fuelling of anti-Muslim racism; the very antithesis of the principles underlying the promotion of cultural development.

The prime minister's reference to separate or parallel lives was a deliberate echo of Ted Cantle's review (Cantle, n.d.) of the causes of major rioting in several northern towns in 2001. Cantle argued that many of those in Britain's Asian community lived almost completely separate lives from their white counterparts – as did, one might argue, many of the white population. As a result, Cantle advocated a new vision of cohesion supported by a range of initiatives designed to translate it into lived reality. Cantle offered an intercultural paradigm that, in his view, is better geared to meet the challenges of our era of globalization and super-diversity than what he described as the old, failed multicultural model. As a guidance exemplar, Cantle cited the Baring Foundation's definition of interculturality as 'a dynamic process by which people from different cultures interact to learn about and question their own and each other's cultures. Over time this may lead to cultural change. It recognizes the inequalities at work in society and the need to overcome these. It is a process which requires mutual respect and acknowledges human rights' (Cantle, 2012: 156).

Regardless of one's position in the multicultural/intercultural debate, what is clear is that we are effectively one world with many cultures, and that creative dynamic interaction is at the heart of cultural change and evolution. Our pupils are subject to a wide range of different and sometimes competing cultures with which they have to negotiate in order to retain a strong sense of self in a world of overlapping multiple identities. If we want to secure a cohesive community, to build a common vision, to value and develop positive relationships across all backgrounds, then it is essential that young people are given the space to express their values openly without fear of recrimination, even when these values differ or perhaps conflict. It is equally essential that, within this supportive framework, young people are taught to be reflectively self-critical and compassionate. Such approaches will help to build what Ostberg (1998) has called 'an integrated plural identity', an identity that allows a young person to feel safe and secure in a range of different settings, an identity in which they are encouraged to become, to adapt Ballard's term, 'skilled and *compassionate* cultural navigators' (cited in Coles, 2007: 27).

Denise Cush (2011) has developed such an approach to religious education, which she calls 'positive pluralism'. This approach encourages pupils to reflect critically on their beliefs and values in the light of what they learn about the religion and cultures of others. Cush argues that in this way pupils can learn from each other without necessarily losing their own religious and cultural roots. She utilizes Mal Leicester's concept of 'limited relativism' – 'accepting that whereas some things are relative to time, location and culture, there is the possibility of overarching shared values such as social justice, human rights, concern for the future and fighting racism which are however continuously negotiated and refined' (cited in Coles, 2007: 28).

The implications for schools: Curriculum, pupils and school culture

Curriculum

The curricular implications of developing systemic 'positive pluralism' in this age of hyper-diversity are profound. Ideally, schools could adopt and adapt as guiding principles 'A Declaration on Cultural Diversity', found in the Parekh Report, *The Future of Multi-Ethnic Britain* (2000: 277). Similarly, they might choose to use the 20 Big Curriculum Questions, a set of overarching principles originally developed by the CREAM (Curriculum Reflecting the Experience of African Caribbean and Muslim Pupils) project team, as funded by the Department for Education and Skills (DfES), to underpin race equality and community cohesion. These principles have been adapted in a range of contexts, including in National Strategies and the Faith and Interfaith Project. The latest version of the questions given below takes account of hyper-diversity, the compassionate taxonomy and the duty on schools to promote cultural development, and can easily be used either as an evaluation exercise or as a form of professional development.

20 BIG CURRICULUM QUESTIONS
1. Commonalities

Does the curriculum stress, at the same time as it depicts diversity of culture and experience, that all people share common aspirations, needs and concerns by virtue of their humanity? For example, does it teach about similarities and common humanity when depicting aspects of British Muslim culture and experience?

2. Diverse perspectives

Does the curriculum teach that, with regard to every event, there are a variety of perceptions, interpretations and perspectives? For example, does it teach about perceptions, outlooks and experiences of Britain's African-Caribbean and African heritage peoples?

3. Diversity within diversity

Does the curriculum counteract over-simplified, stereotypical views by teaching that, within every cultural tradition, there is a diversity of viewpoints, lifestyle and beliefs? For example, does it show that there are many differences within Eastern European culture and experience?

4. Narratives

Does the curriculum teach that every culture interprets its history and learning through certain grand narratives and that these, in turn, contribute to the identities of individuals? For example, does it depict key narratives in the contribution of the citizens of the whole British Empire and Commonwealth to the two world wars?

5. Multiple identities

Does the curriculum teach that most people have a range of affiliations, loyalties and feelings of belonging, and that how these are expressed may change according to context? For example, does it illustrate that all of us assume different roles and behaviour patterns within different settings and readily switch between them?

6. Skilled and compassionate cultural navigators

Does the curriculum actively help young people to navigate with empathy and compassion the tricky waters of living in a range of cultures and sub-cultures?

7. Status and credibility

Does the curriculum give status to the experiences and achievement of people from all backgrounds, cultures and faiths in terms that pupils value? For example, does it acknowledge the considerable contributions of white working-class men and women to the common good and wealth of this nation?

8. Tackling racism, sexism and other prejudices

Does the curriculum teach about issues of racism, for example distinctions between colour racism and cultural racism and between personal and institutional? Does it cover sensitive topics like countering Islamophobia and anti-Semitism?

9. Dynamic culture

Does the curriculum teach that societies and their cultures are constantly changing and developing? Does it teach that there is not a fixed, static view or perspective for a cultural group in any time or place? For example, is the demography of Britain studied to show how, throughout history and today, British identity is shaped by the constant flow of people and ideas?

10. Controversial issues

Does the curriculum sensitively cover issues that might arouse differing opinion such as homosexuality, creationism and responses to radicalization?

11. Interdependence and borrowing

Does the curriculum teach that all learning and human achievement is dependent upon the prior learning/achievement of others and often builds upon and borrows from other cultural traditions? For example, does history teaching recognize how much scientific knowledge commonly attributed to Renaissance discovery was actually an evolutionary development of earlier Islamic thinking?

12. Positive role models

Does the curriculum depict people from a range of cultures and backgrounds achieving eminence as inventors, entrepreneurs, leaders and artists, and demonstrating creativity, initiative and moral courage? For example, are Hindu pioneers and achievers given a place of significance?

13. Normal not exotic

Does the curriculum show that diversity is an aspect of contemporary experience and ordinary, daily life, not merely a feature of distant lands? For example, do pupils learn about everyday Muslim experience in Britain today?

14. Excellence everywhere

Does the curriculum teach that excellence is not restricted to the achievements of people within dominant cultures, but that people in all cultures, today and in the past, achieve excellence?

15. Inclusion

Does the curriculum specifically promote a culture of inclusion, teaching that all people of all cultures and backgrounds are of value and their ideas worthy of consideration?

16. Youth empowerment and service

Does the curriculum help empower young people to work together to embrace difference, to campaign for change and acknowledge diversity, while working towards increasing cohesion and harmony in our society? Does it reinforce the idea of service so that the needs of others in our community are met?

17. United Nations Convention on the Rights of the Child

Does the curriculum teach young people about the global importance of the 54 articles enshrined in this charter?

18. Global perspectives

Does the curriculum teach that we are one world with many cultures and that what happens in one part of the world may well influence us? For example, are young people aware that a contagious outbreak in one country can have adverse effects everywhere?

19. Climate

Does the curriculum cover the global climate crisis with a view to raising awareness that everybody can play some part, no matter how small, in trying to address it?

20. The Golden Rule

Does the curriculum teach young people that the twenty-first-century version of the Golden Rule, 'Treat others and Mother Earth as you would wish to be treated', is common to all faiths and humanist traditions? Does it support young people to act compassionately and become forces for good, drivers of love in action?

Pupils

Effective whole-school implementation of the principles underpinning the 20 Big Curriculum Questions will support the school in its drive to produce culturally developed pupils, but how will schools know if they have been successful? What sort of skills, attitudes and knowledge will young people demonstrate if the curriculum is permeated with the principles? Ofsted offers a descriptive list against which schools are judged. The version below owes much to Ofsted but is enhanced by the work of the Runnymede Trust (2003), whose three-fold format (knowledge and understanding, skills, attitudes) has been adopted. To these, we have added aspects drawn from the CoED Foundation's taxonomy of compassion. We have highlighted in bold the characteristics that are common to cultural development and the taxonomy.

Pupils (and one might add staff) who are becoming culturally aware will be developing some or all of the following knowledge and understanding, skills and attitudes.

KNOWLEDGE AND UNDERSTANDING
- Knowledge and understanding of the influences that have shaped their own cultural heritage, and of the ways in which these both foster and limit one's own personal identity
- Knowledge and understanding of the different cultural traditions within Britain, Europe and the wider world
- An understanding that cultures are not static but are dynamic, and evolutionary

SKILLS
- An ability to **appreciate** cultural diversity and accord dignity and **respect** to other people's values and beliefs
- An ability to go beyond mere tolerance of others to that which celebrates commonalities and differences
- An ability to recognize, **reflect** upon and understand their own cultural assumptions and values
- An ability to contribute to one's own cultural traditions, including the traditions of mainstream public, cultural and political life
- An ability to learn from different cultural experiences, norms and perspectives, and **to empathize** with different traditions
- An ability to analyse and **challenge** features of cultural traditions and to identify instances of prejudice, intolerance and discrimination
- An ability to engage in discussion, argument and negotiation with people for traditions other than one's own
- An ability to **be creative** in a range of contexts – for example, in music, art, literature and architecture; and in religion and politics – which have significance and meaning in a culture

ATTITUDES
- A willingness to be **open** to new ideas
- A willingness to modify cultural values in the light of experience, to turn 'a stream of fresh and free thought upon our stock notions and habits ...'

- A willingness to **appreciate** the diversity and interdependence of cultures
- A willingness to be **open** to a sense of personal enrichment through encounters with cultural media and traditions from a range of cultures
- A willingness to participate in, and respond to, artistic and cultural, sporting, mathematical, technological, scientific and cultural opportunities
- A willingness to show **respect** for 'the best which has been thought and said (and done) in the world'
- A willingness to **challenge** instances of prejudice, intolerance and discrimination
- A willingness to explore and show **respect** for cultural diversity as demonstrated by attitudes towards different religious, ethnic and socioeconomic groups in the local, national and global communities
- A willingness to promote the equalities agenda actively
- A willingness to engage in reasoned discussion concerning controversial issues and come to balanced judgements
- A willingness to accept reasonable and **equitable** procedures for resolving conflicts

School culture

Schools also have their own cultures, their own ways of behaving, of doing things based upon what they value most. So, what would a school look like that was promoting compassionate cultural development? As our baseline, we have amended and added to Ofsted's very useful list (2004).

Encouraging pupils' cultural development

Schools that are encouraging pupils' cultural development are likely to:

- **be clear** about the aims and characteristics of cultural development; how these permeate an inclusive curriculum and how they impact on young people
- **be explicit** in their values, moral purpose and compassionate ethos
- **be aware of** and articulate the impact of cultural development
- **provide experiences** that help young people explore, understand and transcend their own cultural backgrounds
- **provide opportunities to explore** the attitudes, values and traditions of the diverse cultures that make up the UK and the world
- **provide opportunities** for young people to develop the necessary knowledge and understanding, skills and attitudes **to become skilled compassionate cultural navigators**

- **provide a range of creative opportunities** in the Arts, including literature, drama, music, crafts, design and digital technologies
- **provide opportunities** for young **people to attend and reflect** upon a wide range of cultural events
- **provide opportunities to nurture** and develop young people's particular gifts and talents
- **develop a compassionate culture** within which all pupils feel valued, respecting themselves, each other and those who are different
- **develop partnerships** with outside agencies and individuals to extend pupils' cultural awareness, for example supplementary schools, theatre, museum, concert and gallery visits, artists in residence, foreign exchanges
- **address discrimination** on the grounds of race, religion, gender, sexual orientation, age and other criteria and promote racial and other forms of equality.

Conclusion

Cultural development is a circular process. It involves creatively transmitting the school's own cultural values, their ways of seeing and believing and behaving, with those of the wider society. What and how teachers teach is affected by their pupils' needs and the cultural capital they bring. It is a dynamic interactive process, which, for both staff and pupils, involves the cultivation of a perspective, an attitude and a way of seeing the world, each other and the curriculum as a vehicle for connecting and enhancing us. It requires the conscious implementation within the classroom of key characteristics (outlined above) that will support young people in the development of their identity. Compassionate cultural development will enhance pupil interconnectivity, their sense of the self and what has made them, and sharpen their understanding of the responsibilities they will bear for the future.

Let us finish where we began, with C.S. Lewis. By the time their compulsory schooling ends, we would hope that pupils would feel inspired to say that their own eyes were not enough for them, that they too became a thousand people and yet remained themselves. For then, 'as in worship, in love, in moral action, and in knowing' they would transcend themselves and yet would never be more themselves than when they did.

Chapter 6

Compassion through development of physical and mental health and well-being
John Lloyd

Abstract

The Marmot Review, *Fair Society, Healthy Lives* (Marmot *et al.*, 2010), recommended that schools, families and communities should 'work in partnership to reduce the gradient in health, well-being and resilience of children and young people' (18). I argue in this chapter that compassionate education and compassionate schools are central to achieving good physical, mental and emotional health and well-being.

A compassionate school is a healthy school in as much as it promotes and develops health literacy in the young, whereby they are able to assess and evaluate information, managing risk and making lifestyle choices that develop and maintain healthy lifestyles and, ultimately, good health. A compassionate school also promotes the health and well-being of its entire staff, recognizing that a healthy workforce is more likely to be effective in the delivery of high-class teaching and the management of behaviour as well as the relationships necessary to be effective at every level.

In this chapter I examine how schools can be health promoting, where outcomes for health and well-being are the driver; where outcomes prescribed by Public Health England (PHE), the non-statutory curriculum for personal, social, health and economic education (PSHE), along with the personal development outcomes of resilience, mindfulness, self-confidence and self-esteem, are seen as important. I acknowledge the importance of the student voice, where pupils' views and concerns are listened to and acted upon, and where their own participation is valued as they develop political literacy (QCA, 1998).

The chapter references the 10 Principles of PSHE Education (PSHE Association, 2013) and the values that implicitly and explicitly underpin the curriculum in developing a compassionate school. It draws upon what is currently perceived to be good practice by Ofsted (2013), the PSHE

Association (2013) and others, and reflects on the challenges faced by schools in an environment driven by examination results.

Introduction

The importance of the general health and well-being of the population at large has been consistently highlighted in recent years (e.g. Marmot *et al.*, 2010). It is recognized that children and young people are especially vulnerable to lifestyles that, in the short and long term, can lead to physical and mental issues concerning their health and well-being as they grow into adulthood. However, the importance and valuing of the role of schools in promoting health and well-being has diminished.

The Coalition government's White Paper on education recognized that 'children can benefit enormously from high quality Personal Social Health and Economic (PSHE) education', noting that good PSHE 'supports individual young people to make safe and informed choices', as well as tackling 'public health issues' (DfE, 2010a: para 4.30). The White Paper on the government's strategy for public health went further, noting that 'good schools understand well the connections between pupils' physical and mental health, their safety and their educational attainment' (DH, 2010: para 3.16). It argues that 'good schools will be active promoters of health in childhood and adolescence, because healthy children with high self-esteem learn and behave better at school' (para 3.16), and that schools should strengthen young people's 'ability to take control of their lives, within clear boundaries, and help reduce their susceptibility to harmful influences' (para 3.17).

Paradoxically, having blocked the previous government's education bill that would have made PSHE a statutory subject in the curriculum (MacDonald, 2009) and having set out this agenda in the White Paper, the Department for Education (DfE) then withdrew funding and support for the national PSHE continuing professional development (CPD) programme, the Social and Emotional Aspects of Learning (SEAL) programme. It also withdrew funding and recognition for the National Healthy Schools Programme and its accreditation (although the online Healthy School Tool Kit is still available), and marginalized the statutory duty placed on schools to promote well-being (DCSF, 2007). Furthermore, following the DfE's review of PSHE (DfE, 2013b) – undertaken outside the consultation on the new National Curriculum in 2013 (DfE, 2013c) – PSHE remains non-statutory. As such, it is only required of schools that they 'should make provision for personal, social, health and economic education (PSHE), drawing on good practice' and that 'schools are also free to include other subjects or topics of their choice in planning and designing their own programmes of education' (DfE, 2014b: para 2.5).

Given that academies and free schools can choose not to follow the prescribed National Curriculum in England, this hardly counts as an entitlement and, as schools rushed to improve their pupils' academic attainment, it is hardly surprising that lip service is paid to the need for high-quality PSHE, taught by well-trained, confident and competent teachers. It is no surprise either, then, that in its report, *Not Yet Good Enough*, Ofsted (2013) showed that PSHE required improvement in 40 per cent of schools while leadership and management required improvement in a further 42 per cent.

This is somewhat ironic given that the report also notes that, 'there is a close correlation between the grades that the schools in the survey were awarded for overall effectiveness in their last section 5 inspection, and their grade for PSHE education. All but two of the schools graded outstanding at their last section 5 inspection were also graded outstanding for PSHE education and none were less than good' (Ofsted, 2013: 6). This fits well with the findings of a recent research report for the Department for Education (Childhood Wellbeing Research Centre, 2012: 3), which states that:

> Children with higher levels of emotional, behavioural, social and school well-being on average have higher levels of academic achievement and are more engaged in school, both concurrently and in later years.

This is the context in which I portray a compassionate school as one that promotes the physical, emotional and mental health and well-being of children and young people.

A compassionate school promotes health literacy

The notion of 'health literacy' is not new (Kickbusch, 2008; Kickbusch *et al.*, 2006; Sihota and Lennard, 2004; Hodge, 2011) but the term has increasingly come to mean more than being able to read what's on the medicine label and follow the instructions. Nutbeam (2008: 2072) argues that 'Health literacy represents the cognitive and social skills which determine the motivation and ability of individuals to gain access to, understand and use information in ways which promote and maintain good health.' For children and young people to achieve health literacy as an educational outcome, they need through their education and schooling to be able to assess and evaluate information, manage risk and make lifestyle choices that develop and maintain healthy lifestyles and ultimately good health (Lloyd, 2013).

Furthermore, Article 24 of the United Nations Convention on the Rights of the Child states unequivocally that 'Every child has the right to the best possible health. Governments must provide good quality health care, clean water, nutritious food and a clean environment so that children can stay healthy. Richer countries must help poorer countries achieve this' (UNICEF, 1989).

The environment in which this should take place is a school that promotes health and well-being in all it does, not just through the curriculum and PSHE. The school as a setting for health promotion has long been recognized (EC, 1989). The subtle messages pupils receive about health from the daily life of a school are as important as those given in lessons (NCC, 1990). A healthy school (DH, 2005) demonstrates a whole-school approach involving the whole community, providing a curriculum that includes sex and relationship education, drugs education (including alcohol and tobacco), healthy eating, physical activity, and emotional health and well-being (including bullying in all its insidious forms). This is as important for all those employed in schools as it is for the children and young people being taught.

A compassionate school will ensure that policies for sex and relationship education, drugs education, child protection/safeguarding, and confidentiality are up to date and relevant to the needs of pupils and staff throughout the school. Such a school will involve external agencies and health professionals appropriately and make use of local data to inform practice and, where necessary, referral. It continues to be of paramount importance that young people learn how to make healthy food choices in an environment where healthy food and drink are available as part of a school food policy that involves both pupils and staff. Only then will we tackle the obesity crisis and the attendant ill health caused by it. In this regard, the evidence from the Health and Social Care Information Centre (HSCIC, 2014) is of great concern:

> The National Child Measurement Programme (NCMP) measures the height and weight of around one million school children in England every year, providing a detailed picture of the prevalence of childhood obesity. The latest figures for 2013/14, show that in Reception (aged 4–5) 22.5% of children were overweight of which 9.5% of children were obese. Of children in Year 6 (aged 10–11), around 33.5% were overweight or obese. Obesity prevalence among Year 6 children in areas in the most deprived decile was 24.7% compared with 13.1% among those attending schools in the least deprived decile.
>
> (HSCIC, 2014)

A compassionate school will work with pupils and their parents/carers to address this concern and to ensure that children and young people are encouraged to participate in a range of physical activities and to understand how such activity is beneficial to health and mental well-being. Physical activity in this context refers not only to structured activity in the curriculum through physical education and sport, but also those other physical leisure activities available in school and in the community. Any enjoyable activity that encourages young people to be warm and breathless for significant periods of time, and helps them to overcome the barriers to participation brought about by disability, gender, religion and culture, should be valued. Schools still focus too much on traditional team games, which include few and exclude so many. As Mick Waters (2013: 15) notes:

> The euphoria over the 2012 Olympic Games led to the announcements on competitive sport in primary schools being made compulsory. The politicians probably thought this captured a public mood but almost immediately various well-known people came forward to recount their purgatory in school sports as youngsters. Top competitors talked about the joy of sport being derived from its many health and social benefits. Leading coaches described enjoying sport for its own sake and then, gradually, specializing as appropriate. Yet the government grabbed the compulsory and competitive elements and waved the wrong end of the stick as if it were a javelin.

Underpinning all this is emotional health and well-being, both an outcome and a cornerstone of compassionate education and a compassionate school; a school that promotes positive health and well-being, helps pupils to understand and express their feelings, builds their confidence and self-esteem, developing pupils' emotional resilience and their capacity to learn. As the National Institute for Health and Care Excellence (NICE, 2013: 1) maintains:

> Social and emotional well-being creates the foundations for healthy behaviours and educational attainment. It also prevents behavioural problems (including substance misuse) and mental health problems. That is why it is important to focus on the social and emotional well-being of children and young people.

The compassionate school will identify vulnerable children and families and provide pastoral support to help them prioritize healthy behaviour and improve their mental health and well-being (DH, 2012 and 2013). It is appalling that the government discontinued the SEAL programme in 2011, when it had done so much to build positive attitudes to learning and behaviour through building self-esteem and self-confidence, developing empathy for others and making explicit the values underpinning emotional literacy in the classroom. SEAL enabled schools to tackle bullying, harassment and discrimination of every kind, going beyond the obligatory school policy so as to include institutional bullying and discrimination of the work force.

> Pupils' understanding of diversity, prejudice and discrimination was not developed well enough in one in four primary schools and one in eight secondary schools. Pupils had learnt about racism and sexism but not about other forms of discrimination, resulting in their failure to appreciate the impact on others of derogatory language, particularly homophobic and disablist comments. It was evident in responses to the online survey that schools are not doing enough to ensure that pupils have a good awareness and understanding of *all* forms of diversity and discrimination. Almost two thirds of panellists had learnt about racism, just under a half about faith discrimination but only one third had learned about homophobic behaviour and its impact.
>
> (Ofsted, 2013: para 39)

A compassionate school recognizes that a healthy work force – where respect, empathy and genuineness are accorded to all staff and pupils, where teachers are valued as individuals, mutual dependence is fostered and encouraged, and all are open and honest in their dealings with each other – is more likely to be effective in the delivery of high-class teaching and the management of behaviour and relationships that is conducive to good mental health and well-being at every level.

A settings approach

In 'giving children the best start in life', schools and the curriculum have to be seen as a health asset. It is essential that local and national data be used to set priorities at a school and college level as well as regionally and nationally. Schools and colleges have the potential to be important health-promoting settings for children and their families, though not the only ones. That Directors of Public Health in local authorities and local well-being boards make use of ChiMat (Child and Maternal Health Observatory) data and the new School Health Hub would appear to be central to this. The difficulty is engaging with schools in a context where local authority advisers with remits for health and healthy schools have mostly disappeared following funding cuts (the National Healthy Schools Programme has been discontinued as a nationally funded and accredited award). The establishment of academies and free schools, and local and national educational priorities more narrowly focused upon attainment, have not helped. However, as Professor John Newton, Chief Knowledge Officer of PHE, stated unequivocally at the EUSUHM conference in London in June 2013 'schools remain fabulous settings for health improvement and intervention' (Newton, 2013).

Public Health England priorities for children and young people's well-being are: tackling obesity, exercise, mental health, sexual health, alcohol, drugs, the development of skills (recognizing and managing risk, decision-making, knowing where and how to access help, advice and services, resilience). To this end, it is an imperative to reinvigorate a whole-school approach to health and well-being. However, relying on a traditional PSHE curriculum derived from what experts, teachers and other professions believe all children should learn is not necessarily the approach that a compassionate school might take in becoming a health-promoting setting. A one size fits all PSHE curriculum does not actively engage with the reciprocal partnership that should exist between education and health. Local health boards and commissioners should be working with schools to help them make the health and well-being of young people part of their core business, so that the health and well-being of children is perceived as universal and can be targeted as part of a broader public health agenda and approach.

A compassionate school that takes a whole-school settings approach will use national and local data to identify needs, working with health professionals to identify and prioritize the specific needs of young people in the community. Most importantly, actively involving and engaging children and young people, together with their families, in the identification and articulation of their own perceived needs is the mark of a compassionate school. It is vital that pupils' own views and concerns are listened to and acted upon, where their active participation is valued as they develop political literacy (QCA, 1998). Young people cannot be seen as passive learners. Rather, if the outcomes set out for a compassionate school are to be achieved, they have to be encouraged to be contributors and partners in their own learning as they grow and develop and become independent. 'Every child has the right to say what they think in all matters affecting them, and to have their views taken seriously' (UNICEF, 1989, Article 12).

It is ironic that recent reforms to education make children ever-more dependent upon their teachers and the narrow curriculum prescribed by the government rather than encouraging and developing an empowering independence that would befit them well for life beyond school, further study, apprenticeship, higher education or work.

To be targeted and effective, schools need to use approaches that not only match the needs of their pupils but also draw upon evidence of what works in bringing about changes in lifestyles and behaviour. An example of such an approach can be drawn from the Alcohol Education Trust's Talk About Alcohol programme (AET, 2011) for secondary schools, which was evaluated by the National Foundation for Educational Research. The two-year evaluation followed 4,000 pupils in 30 schools and concluded that, as a result of engaging in the intervention programme:

> ... significantly fewer students who had received the intervention had ever had an alcoholic drink by the end of Year 9 compared to students who had not received the intervention (49 compared with 63 per cent). This suggests that the intervention was having an impact on delaying the onset of drinking for this age group. Students who had received the intervention scored significantly higher on questions assessing their knowledge about alcohol and its effects than the comparison students.
>
> (Lynch *et al.*, 2013)

Similarly, work undertaken in Shropshire using the locally produced relationships and sex education resource *Respect Yourself* (Cruttwell, 2012), for use with Years 6 to11, showed that young people reported that they had had significantly increased their confidence, knowledge and networks of support.

In terms of general outcomes for health and well-being, as they move through school and into adulthood, children and young people should:

- demonstrate high self-esteem, a strong sense of personal identity and resilience
- make healthy lifestyle choices for themselves and those for whom they have a responsibility
- assess and take managed risks, protect their own safety and take responsibility for the protection and safety of others.

And for relationships, they should:

- understand and relate well to others and form healthy relationships
- understand and manage conflict

- positively manage their feelings and emotions
- respect others and act with integrity.

This implies a concern for a new set of '3 Rs' in the compassionate school: relationships, risk and responsibility, which will lead to personal development outcomes such as resilience, mindfulness, self-confidence and self-esteem.

Relationships, risk and responsibility

Relationships are central to physical, emotional and mental health. The ability to manage relationships with a wide range of people is essential to the achievement of the core outcomes and should accommodate differences between people of different race, religion, culture, ability or disability, gender, age or sexual orientation, as well as the strong feelings and emotions often present.

Risk and taking risks is part of everyday life. The ability to recognize, assess, respond to and manage risk in relation to health and well-being, the physical environment, relationships, personal finance and the world of work in order to be safe is essential to the outcomes above and must be seen as a means for undertaking new experiences and challenges safely.

Responsibility is learned and assumed as we grow and mature into adults. The ability to listen actively, empathize and understand the consequences of behaviour, to make informed decisions with confidence, and to accept responsibility for actions, is central to the desired outcomes. Only then can one be responsible for oneself and take responsibility for others.

What we know about child and adolescent development and our understanding of health-related behaviour can be distilled into Ten Principles developed by the PSHE Association (PSHE, 2013) and that apply to the whole of PSHE in both primary and secondary schools. These evidence-based principles underpin good practice across Key Stages 1 to 4. How a compassionate school might use these is italicized – my italics.

These principles should be enshrined in curriculum planning for PSHE:

1) Start where children and young people are: *ask them, respond appropriately to their questions, use draw and write* (McWhirter, 2014), *focus groups, questionnaires and make use of locally available data.*

2) Plan a 'spiral programme' which introduces new and more challenging learning: *not repetitive but developmental, showing progression.*

3) Take a positive approach which does not attempt to induce shock or guilt: *this deals with and manages risk and challenge and develops resilience.*

4) Offer a wide variety of teaching and learning styles: *this recognizes the benefits of class teaching, work in small groups, individual work as well as role play, simulations, drama.*

5) Provide information that is realistic and relevant: *use data about young peoples' behaviour that challenges and provides a normative approach.*

6) Encourage young people to reflect on their learning: *this offers self-reflection and regular assessment of work, shows progress; in secondary schools, offer accreditation through ASDAN, OCR and AQA.*

7) Recognize that the PSHE programme is just one part of what a school can do: *this offers opportunities for personal development across and beyond the school curriculum, character-building activities, opportunities to participate.*

8) Embed PSHE education within other efforts: *this recognizes the opportunity for effective PSHE through cross-curricular approaches.*

9) Provide opportunities for children and young people to make real decisions: *this recognizes the influences – their friends, the media, and social networks – on their decision making.*

10) Provide a safe and supportive learning environment: *this deals with misbehaviour, harassment and bullying.*

Answering children's questions

Regarding questioning, the teacher will need the skill to recognize the type of question being asked and to respond appropriately. Some teachers rely upon *question boxes* in which pupils submit their questions anonymously, the teacher then sifts through these and gives answers as a class activity. No matter how they are raised, however, teachers do need to consider the type of question being asked:

- Is it a question that demonstrates the pupil's response to something he/ she does not understand?
- Is it a question that suggests that the pupil has some knowledge of the issue and is seeking clarification?

- Is it a question that suggests that the pupil knows the answer but wants affirmation?
- Is it a question that can be answered for the benefit of the whole class or does it require an individual response later?
- Is it a question that suggests that the pupil has inappropriate knowledge/ beliefs or a personal disclosure that may need following up in line with the school's safeguarding policy (e.g. racist, sexual or criminal)?
- Is it a question that is personal, designed to embarrass the teacher and/ or make the class laugh?
- Is it a question that is intended to elicit personal information from the teacher?

The teacher needs to know how to respond to the last three question types in particular so as to follow them up appropriately.

These principles set a universal standard for the quality of PSHE provision and will be indicative of the achievement of the core outcomes for learners as it relates to their overall health and well-being. The quality of PSHE provision, teaching and learning is critical to the outcomes.

According to Ofsted, schools inspected that had outstanding PSHE had the following characteristics in common, which are consistent with and compatible with the Ten Principles listed above:

> Pupils demonstrate excellent personal and social skills; they share a sense of pride in the contribution they make in school. They can describe what they have learned in PSHE with maturity and enthusiasm, are independent learners and take responsibility. Teachers have excellent subject knowledge and skills and teaching activities meet the needs of different groups and individuals. Teachers are skilful in teaching sensitive and controversial topics and use questioning effectively. They assess learning rigorously. The curriculum is innovative and creative and is regularly reviewed and revised. It is designed to meet the specific needs of disabled pupils and those with special educational needs and those in challenging circumstances. High-quality enrichment activities make an outstanding contribution to the development of PSHE education skills. *Significantly*, school leaders champion PSHE education and both leaders and managers rigorously monitor the quality of teaching.
>
> (Ofsted, 2013: paras 66–80)

Health and well-being and achievement: Two sides of the same coin

These characteristics should also be the mark of a compassionate school. High-quality PSHE and high attainment and achievement are not mutually exclusive. A study carried out by the University of the West of England of over half a million pupils found that young people who passed the ASDAN Certificate of Personal Effectiveness (CoPE), which has significant PSHE within it, raised their chances of achieving A* to C grades in English by 10 per cent and of achieving five A* to C grades, including English and Maths, by 5 per cent. The impact was most significant on those in less privileged groups (Harrison *et al.*, 2012).

These findings confirm that pupils' work towards initiatives such as CoPE doesn't come at the expense of core academic subjects but can, in fact, assist attainment in them. More recently Public Health England (PHE, 2014: 1), supported by the National Association of Head Teachers (NAHT), has made the link between pupil health and well-being and attainment robustly: 'promoting the health and wellbeing of pupils and students within schools and colleges has the potential to improve their educational outcomes *and* their health and wellbeing outcomes'.

Aimed at headteachers, school governors and staff in education settings, the briefing succinctly covers the scientific evidence highlighting the link between health and well-being and educational attainment. It underlines the value for schools of promoting health and well-being as an integral part of a school effectiveness strategy, and highlights the important contribution of a whole-school approach.

Research by the Joseph Rowntree Foundation (Goodman and Gregg, 2010) underscores the need for effective compassionate education encapsulated in PSHE if young people are to achieve their potential. The research indicated that young people are more likely to do well at GCSE if they:

- have a greater belief in their own ability at school
- believe that events result primarily from their own behaviour and actions
- find school worthwhile
- think it likely that they will apply to, and get into, higher education
- avoid risky behaviour, smoking, cannabis use, anti-social behaviour, truancy, suspension and exclusion
- do not experience bullying.

A compassionate school will do everything in its power to mitigate these risks and provide the compassionate care that every child and young person deserves while in school.

Chapter 7

The compassionate curriculum

Mick Waters

Abstract

This chapter considers what a curriculum for compassion might look like. It builds on the argument for compassion in schools offered in the first chapter by examining the way the school curriculum has developed over time and been influenced by the sway of politics on a global scale. The chapter considers where compassion would fit in the curriculum offer; whether it would replace elements that currently exist and act as an alternative or whether it would complement and integrate with the work schools already do to subtly change the way pupils are prepared to make a difference to the world and support their own futures while allowing them to enjoy the present that is their childhood.

What is the curriculum?

The curriculum is the definition of what we would want our young to learn about to enable them to make that step from family to the outside world successfully. It is the learning we believe will realize the hopes we have for them. Most people see schools as adding to what home and community can offer, a supplement that will help children to grow into competent and confident adults with a sense of integrity, the ability to reflect upon their actions, and the necessary skills to influence others and be part of a bigger community. Most families want their children to be fascinated by the natural world, intrigued by humankind's discoveries and inventions and aware of the way mistakes and failings have shaped our world today. Most want their children to enjoy the creative and the innovative and engage with and enjoy the sporting and cultural. Most want their children to appreciate other cultures, outlooks and orientations. Most want them to be prepared or qualified for whatever jobs or training comes next in their adult life. Most want their children to be excited by learning and eager for it to continue.

Curriculum as defined by nations

Nations, though driven by the same pervading ideas, have come to see the school curriculum as a vehicle for national prosperity through the general ability of their adults and the capacity of the curriculum to differentiate ability in people so that the 'more able' can come to the fore to guide their country's growth and future. Realizing that the most economically successful nations have had a schooling system, they seek to establish schools and then, more recently, have sought to define what children will learn.

A national curriculum is a nation's description of what their children should learn. It should be treasured for it usually defines what a nation believes is the entitlement of every child. Schools need to enact their national curriculum and, again quite recently, governments have sought to make their schools accountable through testing of children. The testing is partial, usually focused upon the national language and mathematics, and the more high stakes the accountability is, the less the national curriculum really matters as the spotlight falls instead on this narrower agenda. What gets tested gets taught; this is the real curriculum, the one that pupils meet.

In recent years, the rise of the testing programmes PISA (Programme for International Student Assessment) and TIMMS (the Trends in International Mathematics and Science Study) has created global competition for governments to prove to their electorates that their policies are successful and, again, the emphasis has been on what is tested. The risk of lip service being paid to the defined curriculum as an entitlement is over-ridden by the need to satisfy the machine of measurable results.

What is measurable becomes more attractive to those who devise curriculum content. This is why knowledge has always been so important; it is fixed and true. We can learn about things and the person being tested will either be right or wrong and can then be graded alongside others.

However, we also know that all of knowledge is not fixed and it is certainly not always true. We know that society needs things beyond the simply testable. The problem is that our schooling systems across the world have been built upon and adapted from their origins. Nowhere seems to have the confidence to say: maybe we have been teaching the wrong things and should re-examine our starting point? This is understandable, given that those making the policy decisions have, by and large, succeeded in the original version and would not want to deny its value. And those who have been unsuccessful in the original version generally accept it was they who were inadequate and want a better version of the original for their own children, especially when the successful tell them they do.

Hence national curriculum decisions around the globe usually resort to debates about what content knowledge is in and out in the measurable sense. They become distorted by testing nationally and internationally and, though they sometimes include subjects where the content is more difficult to measure, such as citizenship or health, the prominence of these 'peripheral' aspects of learning is low; low in status and the values placed upon them.

The curse of PISA and politicians

The PISA tests provide detailed information for governments across the OECD. The analysis is deep and offers a set of hypotheses for the comparative performance of different nations. Across the world, ministers of education use their country's performance in the latest PISA tables as justification for their own ideologically driven policies. Their policies usually have very little to do with the analysis but their introduction is laced with references to the need to do better than other countries. Politicians almost always talk of using examples of good practice from elsewhere or learning from successful jurisdictions. It is as though their own success as a minister relates to their ability in lifting the PISA performance for their own country. Given that most political education ministers are short-term appointments, the tactical changes are seldom likely to make much difference in the long term to outcomes for pupils.

In New Zealand, for example, a country highly regarded for its educational success over time and admired for its work on curriculum development and pedagogic approaches, there is a currently a rush towards the mechanistic high stakes accountability narrow schooling that others have implemented over the last 30 years. This is because the nation, through its media and politics, is calling for a better 'standard' when compared with others.

When so-called developing countries decide to focus upon educational achievement, they look to the leading countries and copy their processes, seemingly not recognizing that these processes have scarcely moved forward since the start of the twentieth century. They usually engage consultants from the so-called developed nations to help them. It is as if a country that wished to develop better communication would begin where we began in the developed world, with messages delivered by animal or bird replaced with some sort of postal system, moving to the telegraph and then the telephone. In the world of communication, those same countries leapfrog through this process, recognizing the potential of the future-orientated modern technology. In learning, however, we seem to need to mimic the practices of the old when the reality is that the benefit of 'traditional' schooling, whether in the United States, China, India, England or France, has its roots not in what is learned but in who was met, the networks and contacts made, during our schooling journey.

Ministers, though, love it all. They talk of the changing world of the twenty-first century and uncertain futures and economic uncertainty and technological revolution. They cry that the education system needs to produce free thinkers, ideas generators, team-workers; adaptable, collaborative, creative, challenge-driven people. Once the applause for their wisdom and vision has died down, it does not take long before they are espousing the importance of 'the basics'; magnifying the importance of spelling, punctuation and handwriting. They want the measurable, the testable and what the last generation endured. It shows they are tough and 'reforming'.

Given the right audience, they agree with all of it. Moral education matters, health education is vital, physical learning is paramount, cultural education is essential. Above it all, though, is an academic education. It sounds good and it sounds as though we should all have it. It sounds even better if it is set against vocational education. In many of the countries of the developed world, vocational education is being vilified as unworthy, while business leaders and economists are calling out for people who can transform the labour market.

Many nations are revisiting their national curriculums. China, for example, has decided that it cannot go on feeding the examinations machine and instead must help its young people to be better communicators and stronger team-workers. Singapore has questioned whether such high academic achievement is worth it without a real commitment to a more rounded education. Their study 'Teach Less; Learn More' (Ng, 2014) emphasizes the importance of 'rounded education'. Nevertheless, governments still demand a generally distorted and unbalanced diet of learning for pupils in their schools.

The entitlement dilemma

The curriculum so often suffers because we do not know whether it is a set of learning expectations for the pupils, an entitlement for every pupil, or a broad map of learning for the teacher. Much of this relates to whether we believe all pupils should be able to achieve. National curriculums for science, for example, are usually written from the perspective of the capable and proficient scientist. If we want good scientists, then they will have to be able to know, do and understand the following. Hence, in an entitlement model, all pupils have to try to learn everything. This assumes all have the ability to do so.

Most nations seem to accept that not everyone has the aptitude, ability or capacity to learn and be proficient in everything. Once we accept the principle that some people have special educational needs, we accept that all are not equally able, so it follows that some will be very able to know, do and understand. These are the ones destined to be proficient scientists, mathematicians, linguists, musicians and geographers. The problem is that, while these have to cover everything, those less able than the best find that they cannot know, do or understand much and become disillusioned and negative, seeing themselves as failures. However, if they are not given the opportunity to study all of each domain, we deny them an entitlement and presume that they will not succeed.

It is often argued that curriculum subjects are false divisions as the real world is not divided into art, geography, science, mathematics; the real world is multifaceted so learning should be too. True, as children are small they see a complex intermingled world, devoid of subjects. With good teaching they start to realize that there are branches of study called history, science, arts, mathematics or languages. As these branches separate, so they overlap. Indeed, the branches separate out into specialisms, say, in science, of biology, chemistry and physics, which, in turn, further sub-divide into microbiology, astrophysics, and electrochemistry. These twigs of learning so overlap that from a distance the tree of knowledge appears almost solid; it is only when close up that we see the differences in each subject. What is different is the 'discipline' of each of the subjects, the way it operates and the way it is studied and extended.

The influence of religion

Religion creates a further variable. In some countries, such as England, religious education is expected but not as part of the national curriculum. In other countries, such as Pakistan, religion is seen as the bedrock of the national curriculum, and the school and the mosque work in tandem to inculcate religious learning. Pakistan, though, was established as a country for a particular religious identity. In other countries – France for instance – secular teaching prevails and religious teaching is expected to take place elsewhere than in schools. Even where included, it is not possible to measure the success of religious teaching except in the gaining of agreed knowledge. Because we persist in valuing *learning about*, we test what has been learned about. Someone graded highly in science may not be a good scientist. Being deeply religious and having a religious outlook and way of life guided by religious principles may not show itself in examination success. Where does religion fit?

Most national schooling systems have an element of religious provision. Religions were keen to establish schools to enable the projection of the religion itself as well as broader learning. The upshot of the global shift of people, particularly through the latter half of the twentieth century, has confused the position of religion and the state. Once predominantly single-religion nations now find themselves home to people from many religions. The terrible ethnic or religious cleansing connected with civil wars might be rare but the separateness of neighbourhoods is pervasive and means that religion in schools assumes importance.

Some countries demand a secular education. France espouses this but ran into trouble a few years back over arguments to do with dress code. Other nations practise a specific religion in schools and encourage pupils to worship. It is the distinction between worship (the learning through) and the study of religion (the learning about) that causes tension. A third element is learning 'how to...' and the engagement in ceremony and understanding and feeling the impact is another tension in religious inclusion in curriculum.

Can a curriculum be compassionate?

So what chance compassionate education; a nebulous sounding concept, so obvious and yet so difficult to define? Naturally, we want compassionate people but does compassion not simply emerge? Is it something that can be taught? Where is the testable bit of compassionate education? If we can't test it, what is there to learn and to teach?

Or could compassion be the next element of the unfolding curriculum story? The school curriculum has emerged over time to include the changes in society developed by the learned people. Might compassion be the next element of the curriculum as the world recognizes its growing importance?

The evolving emphasis of the curriculum

In the so-called developed world each nation's outlook on what should be learned by its young has emerged from the evolution of its society. Most believe that children should learn something of their nation's classical traditions. Where Britain turns to the Greeks or Romans as examples of great civilizations, so the South American, Chinese and Indian cultures have their own version of the classical traditions upon which society is built.

In most national curriculum expectations, there is usually an emphasis upon an age of enlightenment, the discoveries of the patterns, properties and phenomena of the earth. Within these discoveries lie the principles of science and mathematics that remain, with modification and sophistication, until today. While enlightenment took place across the globe, many nations seek the claim of invention. For example, Watt and Vapeur were vying to be the inventors of the steam engine but their respective nations lay claim to the invention, often without mention of the other.

Next comes something about the countries' influence on the world. The history unfolds with claims to just victory in battles and wars, treaties and alliances that have made the nations what they are today.

Many nations have a commitment to having their young understand their governing principles. Where democracy is strong, there are key messages about emancipation and equality or breaks from imperial rules and moves toward independence. Where other forms of government prevail, the story helps to maintain the status quo, encouraging servitude or adherence to the societies' ruling beliefs. In some cases, such as Japan, the nation explicitly teaches its young about the mistakes of the past as a way of atoning for atrocities committed.

Most nations encourage some experience of arts and culture. Firstly, they are such natural forms of expression for the young, and secondly because they are ways to reinforce the stories of the nation's past. The late twentieth century, though, brought with it a creative upsurge that continues to grow exponentially, built upon rapid advances in technology. These advances bring new forms of arts and culture to the young through new and difficult to control media.

In turn, this era of connectedness makes learning so much more accessible and 'modern', leaving governments across the world trying to grapple with the challenge of teaching in traditional schooling systems while the young learn from multiple sources. They expect their schools to pay attention to the global revolution in communication as part of learning without quite knowing what do about it.

The changing world

While the curriculum we see in schools across the world has evolved slowly over time, the world in which the young are schooled has changed dramatically. In the 30 years or so since national curriculums began to emerge in the developed world, employment patterns have diversified, there have been global shifts of population, economic competition between nations has intensified, the planet is smaller in all forms of communication, and life expectancy for many has grown while the gap between rich and poor has become greater.

What counts as success in schools has also changed. Where 30 years ago, only some pupils were expected to succeed at school and go on to help to run their nation, first more, then most and now all are expected to succeed at school. Governments seek the silver bullet that will enable all their pupils to achieve to satisfy electorates that have been convinced that economic success, wealth and prosperity rely on a few academic indicators secured at school. Hence the importance of the PISA tables.

The problem is that governments cannot get away from describing the content of learning in terms that the older generations recall and understand. Whereas most would be dissatisfied with a television or telephone from just ten years ago, politicians resort to description of what needs to be learned by naming those items that are remembered rather than the essence of the learning.

Different ways to describe the content ... compassionately

What is needed is not an overthrow of all that exists but a careful appraisal of why we teach what we do, why we wish our young to experience certain learning and what the long-term benefits are to the nation and the planet of more developed thinking in this way.

If the classical traditions were seen as reason and argument, containing ethics, logic and rhetoric, there would be a resonance in most nations. If young people were to learn of the phenomenon that is our world, and how people have worked to understand it, there would be general agreement. The widening knowledge could support the growth and development of understanding of our world. The creative upsurge is best described as modern-day invention, solution and innovation. Where democracy is the guiding principle then fairness and justice can be explored within an outlook of consideration.

Our previous thinking could be re-examined and reshaped to better reflect our compassionate intentions, which would influence the way we teach, the way young people are asked to learn and the outcomes of that learning.

How is compassion built into a curriculum?

It would not take much of a shift to see the learning that young people do in different terms.

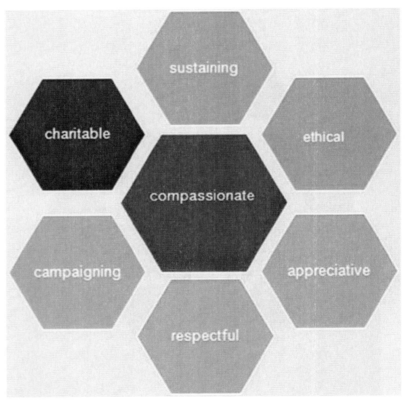

Figure 7.1: Attributes of a compassionate curriculum

These descriptors would be part of a compassionate curriculum. Much content already included in the curriculums of many countries would fit naturally within these descriptors. To drive learning through these dimensions demands a degree of confidence when the results are so hard to measure. It is easier to measure knowledge in subjects such as art, geography or science than to identify development in respectfulness. It sounds soft, whereas academic study is hard.

Striving for compassionate content

The essence of compassion is not that we measure it but that we offer it. Pupils can learn to be compassionate by being engaged in activity through which they learn about the importance of their actions as a human being having integrity; that they should be decent to themselves, to others, their community and to the globe. The measure is in a better world for everyone rather than an examination certificate each. In its root a compassionate curriculum has respect, which can be studied in the context of great matters of history, the working relationships between scientists and their discoveries, and the ways in which our world has been adapted by humans in the quest for a safer or more fruitful existence. In contrast, the lack of respect would be evidenced in historical exploitation, some of the examples of deceit and chicanery that run alongside the scientific steps forward made in society. The understanding that the famous explorers who shaped so much of our knowledge of the planet were often also plunderers, buccaneers and wealth and territory gatherers is one often omitted by the writers of national curriculum documents across the world. As empires grew, so the motives of the notorious heroes from all civilizations come into question. The archaeological finds and the retrieval of discoveries for scientific analysis are seen by many as grave robbery and destruction. The ongoing slavery and subjugation of peoples across the globe, the evils of dictatorship, the effect of apartheid are all worthy elements of learning for pupils with the maturity to deal with the complex issues involved. Equally, the effectiveness of various actions – from blockades, to isolation and boycott – is worth consideration. With a compassionate curriculum goes the willingness to address controversy.

An awareness of injustice might naturally lead to consideration of campaigning for truth, justice and a fairer society. A compassionate curriculum would see pupils studying uprisings, revolts and revolution. Their own life in school would help them to address matters of protest, learning the difference between reasonable and unreasonable protest and understanding how easily extremism can develop. Schools might consider how they would provide vehicles for protest and confrontation of matters in which unreasonable expectations are in place. In 2014 some French pupils came to prominence across the web as teenage males wore skirts to school in protest at the enforcement of dress code regulations. A compassionate curriculum might see the school actively encouraging pupils to be part of campaigning organizations while at the same time promoting study of truth or otherwise behind the claims of some organizations. The protection of the planet, its plants, creatures and people is surely a reasonable aspect of study and through it the applications of mathematics, history and science can only increase the intellectual challenge.

That notion of protection leads to an awareness of sustainability. The world's resources are finite. The challenges of climate change, food and famine, fossil fuel, pollution or population growth are all elements of sustainability that will put learning of many subjects into context for the pupil. Contact with people across the planet will enable pupils to develop an understanding of a shrinking planet and the need for peoples to work together in harmony and joint enterprise to create a more sustainable world. For the Kyoto agreement to be more than rhetoric, the next generation needs to be active and pick up the baton for the challenges ahead for the planet. If this brings pupils to question the roles of governments, big business or ruling classes, some would question its validity. A free world might encourage its young to question aspects of transparency, double standards and deliberate deceit. Politics and power have to be engaged with to be understood. Better understanding might produce a more active and involved population committed to democratic government, and arrest the cynicism seen in nations all over the world when compared with the achievement of other nations celebrating the emancipation of the vote.

In the compassionate curriculum the disciplines of science, history and the arts would complement each other rather than fight for supremacy. They are all interlocking perspectives on human development, all telling a story and offering a joint narrative, sometimes setting out challenges for the future.

It is that awareness of the interlocking but different narratives of the development of civilization through different subject disciplines that will create an appreciation of the world in which we live. Pupils need to be helped to appreciate the reasons why people did as they did in the past. They need to appreciate how throughout the ages people have needed to record their living circumstances, their joy and their despair through art and they in turn have appreciated those gifted among them who are able to record, interpret and challenge through their poetry, painting, song, sculpture or photography. They need to appreciate the scientific discoveries and mistakes. Pupils become aware of the plight of others, whether this means living with limited water for a day, seeing the world through the experience of some of the disabled by spending a day in a wheelchair or trying to cope for a week on limited money. They might also appreciate that the horrors of the natural disasters such as a Haitian earthquake or a Japanese tsunami are different from the horror of a disaster such as the Bhopal gas leak, the collapse of the Rana Plaza clothing factory or the Hillsborough tragedy.

The emphasis upon compassion would naturally lead to the encouragement of charitable behaviours. Linked to campaigning, the taking of positive action to support causes through direct action or funding, whether it be in natural disaster or war, poverty or the preservation of areas of the globe or its creatures that are under threat, a school might take concerted action on the charitable, well thought out and managed as an integral part of its learning agenda. People across the globe were asked to support UNICEF by making a donation during the Commonwealth Games in Glasgow. Millions did. The challenge for schools is to teach that charity is more than being kind to those in need and should not encourage dependency. True charity is about redistribution of resources to give others a fairer opportunity.

The organization of charitable efforts teaches much in the way of soft skills that employers across the globe are seeking. Teamwork, flexibility, determination, empathy and organizational skills emerge through authentic activity for real purposes. Project planning is better learned on a proper project, strategic management makes more sense when it is built around a real strategy, resource management counts when real resources are needed and policy is better appreciated when there is one that matters in place. Stephen Sutton, an English teenager with terminal cancer organized a charitable effort from his sick bed and achieved world-wide recognition for his efforts. (See: www.teenagecancertrust.org/get-help/young-peoples-stories/stephen-sutton.)

Encouraging charitable action in pupils can be more than harnessing the money-raising potential of the school community to build substantial sums for a 'good cause', be it one of the media-popular efforts or support for a local endeavour to ease hardship, help in an emergency or build a facility for local good. Pupils need to be helped to consider the charities' ethics, ways of working and track record of success. By involving them at every level, pupils learn to be discerning about charitable work, its techniques, accomplishments and side effects.

Into all of this comes respect for self, each other, our community and the globe. The subject disciplines are full of examples of ways in which people have or have not demonstrated respect over the course of history. Where land grabbing has started wars, where science has moved forward without heed of consequences, where artists have communicated their lack of respect, so mathematicians, musicians and linguists can point to their own examples of intolerance, belligerence and threat. Instead of pupils being taught about stories of daring-do, resilience and heroism, they might better discover the often untold stories behind the scenes and consider the moral of the stories, about how we might behave. Learning is about the influence on behaviour.

At the personal level, each pupil should learn about their own health and their responsibility towards themselves. Abuse in its many forms threatens to blight the lives of our young. They are at risk from drink, drugs, smoking, sex, lack of exercise, poor diet, internet grooming and, in some places, weaponry. While the world is full of opportunity as never before, the threats are significant. Where typically we try to encourage young people to believe that they can cross thresholds and address what lies on the other side with confidence, these risks point to where we need to teach each individual to know how to avoid being drawn in, how to avoid becoming out of their depth in what began as a curious adventure, and when and how to say stop. The myths, legends and classics of literature in most cultures carry such messages; the young need to be helped to *learn through* such experiences and not simply *learn about* them.

National governments demonstrate their respect or otherwise in their treatment of each other. The tolerance of dictatorships, the willingness to invade other countries based on considerations of economy over human dignity and repression, the holding on to territories irrationally rather than returning them to the most logical control are all examples of matters that pupils might reasonably consider if education has truly the intent of creating a better world. The ongoing story around Malala Yousafzai fascinates most young people. Her campaigning zeal is undimmed by her atrocious injuries. (See: http://www.biography.com/people/malala-yousafzai-21362253#after-the-attack.)

The consideration of ethics takes us forward into the twenty-first century and backward to the nineteenth, since ethics, along with logic and rhetoric, were part of the curriculum of the early public schools. The ethics of scientific methodology, accurate recoding of history, plagiarism in writing or art, and drug use in sport are fundamental concerns going forward, some of which have overtones of the past. Who discovered and laid claim to territory, who 'evolved' new theories (it is a pun and an allusion) and allowed them to be claimed as their own, who treated others badly but might be fondly recalled in statues and portraits would prove worthwhile considerations in serious subject disciplines.

Is the compassionate curriculum a new approach to religious education?

The compassionate curriculum is not a newly stated religious curriculum. It could take learnings from many of the world's religions and these religions could become vehicles for *learning through* and *learning how to* in respect of many aspects of life. Well taught, religion would point to many elements of a compassionate curriculum and many elements of the compassionate curriculum would support the teachings of religions across the world. Humanism would equally have a synthesis with a compassionate curriculum.

So can a compassionate curriculum be structured? Or is it just a pervading idea?

Are the concepts of a compassionate curriculum within the grasp of young minds in schools? Is a compassionate curriculum something that becomes available when a bed rock of knowledge has been laid as a foundation? Or is a compassionate curriculum something that builds from the natural learning of the young child? The concepts can begin early. Most of them can be introduced from a young age, using a *learning through* method. Sustainability takes place through gradually making young children aware of the wastefulness of the planet, whether in energy or food. At that point, they can do something about it, although it may be later that they *learn about* and *learn how to*.

The structure of content to learn within a compassionate curriculum relies on responsibility being taken at all parts of a continuum. At the pupil level, the curriculum can be framed by compassion, and at school level the analysis of the content of subject disciplines can inform and be informed by the compassionate concepts. It is not a case of writing a new curriculum but more of reassessing the message of much of the content to ensure that compassion is a driver. At a national level, schools need their governments to shape a curriculum that encourages a proper compassionate endeavour and then to make it happen through their accountability processes.

It should be possible to teach a global curriculum at an international level. Concepts such as trigonometry, geometry, density and pressure are the same the world over. It will surely not be long before technology is able to help people to *learn how to* use such global concepts effectively. At the same time, the global aspirations of the United Nations Convention on the Rights of the Child need to be realized and nations need to accept their responsibility in this regard. The list of 54 articles could be required learning for pupils across the world. They would *learn through*, *learn about* and *learn how to*, and the learning in schools would become alive with relevant, authentic and embedded experience. Properly embraced by nations, these articles would ensure a compassionate curriculum ... worldwide.

Conclusion: Bringing it all together – The next steps
Maurice Irfan Coles

Compassion is one of the oldest, simplest and most intuitive forces in human history. It is a universal, timeless and radical concept that does not depend on any one culture. It can give our lives a sense of meaning and purpose, and contribute to our health and well-being. Although we are wired for compassion, our old brain psychologies – the cortisone-driven fear and flight mode – serve to undermine our better instinct. The best of world religions, the ancient contemplative traditions and contemporary secular neuroscience, psychology and mindfulness provide significant supportive signposts in our journey towards the compassionate school. Access for young people, however, depends on the context of their upbringing, whom they meet and what they read and watch. What is urgently required is an education system that teaches about compassion, teaches compassionately and encourages 'acts for love': a system, in short, that has collaboration and service as its highest ideals.

On one level this looks like the agenda from hell – another series of impossible burdens that, once again, principals, teachers, support staff and governors are asked to shoulder with no extra resources and no overall direction. But, on another, it looks manageable. Yes, it is a big agenda but it is something schools are already doing in many ways. The trick is to begin to make the compassionate journey *intentional*, to make it *the key organizing principle of school life*. It will, of course, need to be achieved on an incremental basis with each area of school life scrutinized through the prism of compassion.

Education and society's tectonic plates are shifting. They are moving away from a narrow attainment-based, individualistic, consumerist focus to something that stresses collaboration and service. Let us not, however, make our claims too extravagant. Compassion – and compassionate education – is not a magic wand, a panacea for all the world's ills. No such thing exists. It can, however, be the magic wardrobe through which young people can walk to find their own solutions to the problematic legacies we are leaving behind.

Educators have a key role, if not *the* key role in helping to bring this about. This book has tried to provide a theoretical underpinning and practical supportive steps. But how do we know if we have achieved it? What would a compassionate school actually look like?

A compassionate school would exhibit all or some of the following characteristics. It would:

- have compassion as its key ongoing organizing principle, so that it permeates everything the school does
- ensure compassion infuses and enthuses its curriculum content and curricular processes
- ensure compassion forms the bedrock of initial teacher and continuing professional development
- have signed the Charter for Compassion with the Golden Rule at its heart, and with the Golden Thread pulsating through its arteries
- use the taxonomy of compassion, 'acts for love', as a key vehicle for both values transmission and as an audit tool
- have a complete workforce, including school governors and managers, who articulate the vision and live its principles
- have leaders, staff, parents and carers who model these values
- have a pupil population that aspires to these ideals, which will be clearly visible, both in their behaviours and in how they treat each other and adults in the school and beyond
- employ collaborative and co-created processes in classroom, staffroom and parental interactions
- employ pupil, staff and whole-system assessments that do not undermine good practice but build upon it
- enjoy a culture of listening based upon empathetic understanding and a willingness to appreciate the view of the other
- teach pupils some knowledge of how the brain works so that they understand we are wired for compassion
- allow its pupils and staff the space to contemplate, to reflect, to be mindful
- be proactive in its local and wider community
- be proactive in building local, national and international cohesion
- be a health-promoting school that pays due regard to the social, emotional and spiritual aspects of learning
- be a school that really values educating the heart
- be a school that is culturally inclusive and meets the needs of its diverse pupil population
- be a school that safeguards its pupils and teaches them skills to live in this digital age

- practise restorative justice as part of its behaviour policy
- be a school that balances high attainment with high self-esteem
- be a campaigning school, championing the rights of others and the needs of the planet
- celebrate and regularly praise kindness and compassionate acts
- encourage the ideal of service, collegiality and love in action for our global interconnected universe
- be a happy school with lots of smiling faces.

We can sum up the characteristics of the compassionate educator and the compassionate school as 'love in action'. The adoption of this principle in everything we do in school life provides the Golden Thread through which we help young people create a better and more just world. Students must still attain, must develop academic, vocational and social skills, but should have a more balanced purpose of elevating service, rather than self, as the key virtue. If pupils leave our care celebrating the maxim that 'universal compassion is the only guarantee of morality' (Schopenhauer, cited in Dossey, 2013: 6), we will have gone some way to fulfilling our responsibilities to future generations. I end with the words of St Paul (from one of the greatest short tracts ever written) who, in response to the Christian Corinthians' question as to who was the greatest God, argued, simply, that it was love:

> If I speak in the tongues of mortals and of angels, but do not have love, I am a noisy gong or a clanging cymbal. And if I have prophetic powers, and understand all mysteries and all knowledge, and if I have all faith, so as to remove mountains, but do not have love, I am nothing. If I give away all my possessions, and if I hand over my body so that I may boast, but do not have love, I gain nothing.
>
> Love is patient; love is kind; love is not envious or boastful or arrogant or rude. It does not insist on its own way; it is not irritable or resentful; It bears all things, believes all things, hopes all things, and endures all things.
>
> Love never ends. But as for prophecies, they will come to an end; as for tongues, they will cease; as for knowledge, it will pass away When I was a child, I spoke like a child, I thought like a child, I reasoned like a child; when I became an adult, I put an end to childish ways. And now faith, hope, and love abide, these three; and the greatest of these is love.

(1 Corinthians, Chapter 13: 1–13)

Afterword

At a time when the focus in education is on structural change and examinations, it is all too easy to forget about those things that can't be measured and don't find a place on the political agenda. But these things really matter if we are to develop an education service that prepares children for the world in which they will grow to adulthood. Compassion is one of those things. It's a word which, until the beginning of this century, appeared somewhat out of date and out of fashion. But the attitudes and values it encompasses are as relevant now as ever and have come to the fore as one of the most important driving forces in the twenty-first century.

We sometimes make the mistake of thinking that the way people behave to their friends, to strangers and to their community comes naturally and can't be taught. This book shows how mistaken such an assumption is. It argues for compassion to have a central role in how we educate the next generation – in the curriculum, in the way we organize schools and in the messages we give young people about what is important. In this sense, it will stir a debate but at the same time offer very practical ideas as to how this ideal could be turned into reality and the impact it could have.

Estelle Morris, Baroness of Yardley
Former Secretary of State for Education and Patron of the CoEd Foundation

Appendix 1: Charter for Compassion

The following Charter for Compassion is taken from http://charterforcompassion.org/sign-share-charter.

The principle of compassion lies at the heart of all religious, ethical and spiritual traditions, calling us always to treat all others as we wish to be treated ourselves. Compassion impels us to work tirelessly to alleviate the suffering of our fellow creatures, to dethrone ourselves from the centre of our world and put another there, and to honour the inviolable sanctity of every single human being, treating everybody, without exception, with absolute justice, equity and respect.

It is also necessary in both public and private life to refrain consistently and empathically from inflicting pain. To act or speak violently out of spite, chauvinism, or self-interest, to impoverish, exploit or deny basic rights to anybody, and to incite hatred by denigrating others—even our enemies—is a denial of our common humanity. We acknowledge that we have failed to live compassionately and that some have even increased the sum of human misery in the name of religion.

We therefore call upon all men and women to restore compassion to the centre of morality and religion ~ to return to the ancient principle that any interpretation of scripture that breeds violence, hatred or disdain is illegitimate ~ to ensure that youth are given accurate and respectful information about other traditions, religions and cultures ~ to encourage a positive appreciation of cultural and religious diversity ~ to cultivate an informed empathy with the suffering of all human beings—even those regarded as enemies.

We urgently need to make compassion a clear, luminous and dynamic force in our polarized world. Rooted in a principled determination to transcend selfishness, compassion can break down political, dogmatic, ideological and religious boundaries. Born of our deep interdependence, compassion is essential to human relationships and to a fulfilled humanity. It is the path to enlightenment, and indispensable to the creation of a just economy and a peaceful global community.

Appendix 2: Web-based resources

The National and International Compassion in Education Network (NICEN)

The NICEN is an informal web-based list of organizations that can provide compassionate support, training and materials. Many provide their own newsletters and many have written their own books. NICEN has been compiled by the CoED Foundation and is reviewed and updated constantly. The current list can be found at: http://coedfoundation.org.uk/pages/projects_nicen.html. The following NICEN extracts have been loosely clustered according to the respective chapter headings. Several, of course, can be placed in a number of different categories. A brief synopsis of their offering precedes the web links.

Compassion general:

- **Action for Happiness** offers courses and resources to promote happiness and wellbeing: www.actionforhappiness.org.
- **Center for Building a Culture of Empathy and Compassion** aims to build a movement for creating a global worldwide culture of empathy and compassion. It is a portal for resources and information about the values of empathy and compassion. The site contains articles, conferences, definitions, experts, history, interviews, organizations, videos and science: www.facebook.com/EmpathyCenter.
- **The Center for Compassion and Altruism Research and Education (CCARE)**, based at Stanford, is one of the leading centres for compassionate research and dissemination: http://ccare.stanford.edu.
- **Charter for Compassion** has a dynamic website dedicated to all areas of compassion: http://charterforcompassion.org/global-compassion-movement.
- **Empathy and Compassion in Society** is the umbrella group that organizes an annual conference that covers all aspects of compassion. Past conference papers and videos are available: http://compassioninsociety.org.

- **The Fetzer Institute** is a US-based international organization that aims to foster awareness of the power of love and forgiveness in the emerging global community. Its work is grounded in a conviction that the connection between the inner life of spirit and outer life of service and action in the world holds the key to lasting change: http://fetzer.org/about-us.
- **Global Peace Initiative of Women** (GPIW) is an international network of women and men spiritual and community leaders that places a special emphasis on building interfaith understanding and developing leadership in young community leaders worldwide: www.facebook.com/GlobalPeaceInitiativeofWomen.
- **Greater Good: The Science of a Meaningful Life**, based at Berkeley, California, offers a range of articles, courses and conferences dedicated to the science of compassion: greatergood.berkeley.edu.
- **St Ethelburga's Centre for Reconciliation and Peace**, based in London, offers courses, conferences, performances and consultancies aimed to promote peace and understanding: www.stethelburgas.org/about-us.
- **Wisdom 2.0: compassion and mindfulness in the digital age** offers insights into compassion in business: www.wisdom2summit.com/Videos.

Compassionate education general:

- **Charter for Compassion**'s discrete education arm is found at: Charterforcompassion.org/education-book.
- **The Compassionate Mind Foundation**'s school-based initiative at Salt Ash Community School can be found at: www.compassionatemind.co.uk/home/news_1.htm.
- **Compassionate Schools Network** is a free online community inspired by the first ever Compassionate Schools conference, which took place in Seattle in 2014. It offers teachers, parents, students, administrators and community members a space to collaborate, share resources, and find support: www.compassionateschoolsnetwork.org.
- **Creating Compassionate Cultures**, Pam Cayton's online materials: creatingcompassionatecultures.org.
- **The Forgiveness Project** explores rather than propagates forgiveness, reflecting the stories of real people: http://theforgivenessproject.com.
- **The Foundation for Developing Compassion and Wisdom** provides programmes and resources that promote mindfulness and self-awareness and emotional intelligence and resilience: www.compassionandwisdom.org.

- **Friends of the Earth's Youth & Education programme** creates ways for young people to explore: environmental issues; citizenship; sustainable development: www.foe.co.uk/learning/educators/resource_index.html.
- **Global Oneness Project** has been producing and curating multicultural stories since 2006. Each month, they release a new story and an accompanying lesson plan aligned to National and Common Core Standards: www.globalonenessproject.org/about-project.
- **Greater Good**'s discrete education arm is found at: http://greatergood. berkeley.edu/education.
- **Heroic Imagination Project** is a research-based organization that provides knowledge, tools, strategies and exercises to individuals and groups to help them to overcome the social and psychological forces that can keep them from taking effective action at crucial moments in their lives: http://heroicimagination.org.
- **Mind with Heart** is an international charity dedicated to equipping young people with the skills needed for developing character and for building a more sustainable society: http://mindwithheart.org/en/about-us.
- **Non-violent communication (NVC)** is used the world over in schools, prisons, peace processes, organizations, with couples, in families, between friends with an aim to create interactions where the needs of every human being are heard and valued: www.nvc-uk.com/.
- **Oxfam Global Citizenship for Teachers** offers a huge range of ideas, resources and support for developing global learning in the classroom and the whole school. All of the resources here support Education for Global Citizenship – education that helps pupils to understand their world and make a positive difference in it: www.oxfam.org.uk/education/global-citizenship.
- **Peace Mala, project for world peace** is a Welsh-based charity that focuses on the Golden Rule. It offers courses, consultancies, resources and accreditation: www.peacemala.org.uk.
- **Random Acts of Kindness** (RAK) is a worldwide movement with its own foundation, a RAK week and a series of accompanying lesson plans: www.randomactsofkindness.org.
- **REsilience** is a UK-based initiative for teachers of religious education, originally funded by the British government, offering resources and help to develop teacher confidence and competence in dealing with contentious issues in the classroom: www.re-silience.org.uk/index.php.

- **Roots of Empathy programmes** is an evidence-based classroom programme that has shown significant impact in reducing levels of aggression among school children while raising social/emotional competence and increasing empathy: www.rootsofempathy.org/en/what-we-do.html.

Compassionate minds (and brains) in education

- **Body In Mind Training** offers teachers and other professionals courses designed to bring a mindful way of working into the classroom with some gentle teaching but mostly focusing on the teacher's own practice and engagement with mindfulness: www.facebook.com/BodyInMindTraining.
- **Compassionate Mind Foundation** aims to promote wellbeing through the scientific understanding and application of compassion, offering courses, workshops and other materials: www.compassionatemind.co.uk.
- **Compassionate Wellbeing** hosts events, and supports research and activities that promote and explore compassionate approaches to health, wellbeing and society. The work is based on compassion-focused therapy and the compassionate mind Approach: www.compassionatewellbeing.co.uk.
- **Learning to Breathe** is a US programme for late teens. This six-week programme aims to: increase awareness of thoughts, feelings and bodily sensations; reduce harmful self-judgements; and integrate mindful awareness into daily life: http://learning2breathe.org.
- **Mindfulness-based stress reduction (MBSR)** incorporates meditation, yoga and mind–body exercises to help people cope with stress. BeMindful offers online courses and other resources: http://bemindful.co.uk.
- **Mindfulness in Schools Project (MiSP) or .b ('dot be')** is a curriculum-based intervention that aims to incorporate a mindful and compassionate way of teaching: http://mindfulnessinschools.org.
- **MindUP** offers a research-based training protocol for educators and children of various ages, currently available via Scholastic publishers: http://thehawnfoundation.org/mindup.

Compassion through spiritual development

- **The Center for Visionary Leadership**, founded by Corinne McLaughlin and Gordon Davidson, offers a regular e-letter, articles, DVDS and practical help: www.visionarylead.org.

- **Faith, Interfaith and Cohesion: The Education Dimension** offers a comprehensive list of organizations devoted to spiritual and interfaith work. Available at: www.coedfoundation.org.uk.
- **James Redfield's Celestine Vision:** Redfield and his team offer courses, newsletters and resources related to synchronicity: www.celestinevision.com/.
- **Spirituality & Practice** is the well-established, influential site of Frederic and Mary Ann Brussat, who offer courses, conferences and a large range of materials: www.spiritualityandpractice.com.
- **Sufi tradition** is encapsulated in the *Treasury of the Heart* by Sheikh Mahmood Rashid and Maurice Irfan Coles. Available from: www.coedfoundation.org.uk.
- **Transcendental meditation** is a simple, mental technique that allows the mind to transcend, or settle to, the simplest, most powerful state of awareness: http://uk.tm.org/home.
- **The World Community for Christian Meditation** supports the practice of meditation as taught by John Main OSB and Lawrence Freeman OSB. Resources, webcast and training information, reflections as well as school-based work are available: www.wccm.org. In the UK, contact: charles@posnett.entadsl.com.

Compassion through cultural development

- **Black History Month in the UK:** www.blackhistorymonth.org.uk.
- **Black History Month in the USA:** www.history.com/topics/black-history/black-history-month.
- **Curriculum Enrichment For The Future – Discover the Past: Develop the Future:** The curriculum arm of 1001 Inventions: www.ce4tf.org/.
- **Facing History and Ourselves** began in the USA in 1976, and the organization is now found in over 160 countries and has produced a huge range of materials for pupils: www.facinghistory.org.
- **Holocaust Memorial Day:** The following sites offer extensive resources for teachers:
  - www.redcross.org.uk/en/What-we-do/Teaching-resources/Lesson-plans/Holocaust-Memorial-Day
  - www.ushmm.org/educators/lesson-plans
  - http://globaldimension.org.uk/calendar/event/4177
  - http://hmd.org.uk/content/for-educators
  - www.tes.co.uk/article.aspx?storyCode=6065594
- **1001 Inventions: Muslim Heritage in Our World:** www.1001inventions.com.

- *Insted* is a British based organization specializing in equalities, issues related to Islamophobia and Jewish education: www.insted.co.uk.

Compassion though social and moral development and PSHE

- **Collaborative for Academic, Social, and Emotional Learning (CASEL)**, based in the United States, advances the development of academic, social and emotional competence for all students. It aims to make evidence-based Social and Emotional Learning (SEL) an integral part of education from preschool through to high school: www.casel.org.
- **The Jubilee Centre for Character and Virtues** based at the School of Education, University of Birmingham, England, offers a range of courses, consultancies and resources designed to promote character development: www.jubileecentre.ac.uk.
- **Social and Emotional Aspects of Learning (SEAL):** Resources available in the UK: http://webarchive.nationalarchives.gov.uk/20110809101133/nsonline.org.uk/node/87009.

Compassion through action

The following organizations provide online campaigning and petitions:

- **38 Degrees** – people, power, change – a UK based online campaigning community: www.38degrees.org.uk.
- **Avaaz** is an international campaigning organization: www.avaaz.org.
- **change.org** – online petitions at: www.change.org/en-GB.

References

AET (2011) *Talk About Alcohol: Teacher work book for 11 to 18 year-olds.* Alcohol Education Trust. Online. www.alcoholeducationtrust.org/teacherarea/download-teacher-workbook (accessed June 2015).

Armstrong, Karen (2009) TED Global. Online www.ted.com/speakers/karen_armstrong (accessed January 2014).

Arnold, M. (1869) *Culture and Anarchy.* Cambridge: Cambridge University Press.

Barber, M., Donnelly, K. and Rizvi, S. (2012) *Oceans of Innovation.* London: IPPR.

Bei, B., Byrne, M.L., Ivens, C., Waloszek, J., Woods, M.J., Dudgeon, P., Murray, G., Nicholas, C.L., Trinder, J. and Allen, N.B. (2013) 'Pilot study of a mindfulness-based, multi-component, in-school group sleep intervention in adolescent girls'. *Early Intervention in Psychiatry*, 7 (2), 213–20.

Berger, P.L. (2014), *Redeeming Laughter: The comic dimension of human experience.* New York: Walter de Gruyter.

Bishop, S.R., Lau, M., Shapiro, S., Carlson, L., Anderson, N.D., Carmody, J., Segal, Z.V., Abbey, S., Speca, M., Velting, D., Devins, G. (2004) 'Mindfulness: A proposed operational definition'. *Clinical Psychology: Science and Practice*, 11 (3), 230–41.

Brach, T. (2004) *Radical Acceptance: Embracing Your Life With the Heart of a Buddha.* New York: Bantam Books.

Brewer, J.A., Kober, H., Worhunsky, P.D., Tang, Y.-Y., Gray, J.R. and Weber, J. (2011) 'Mental training reveals differences in default mode network activation and functional connectivity'. *Proceedings of the National Academy of Sciences*, 108 (50), 20254–20259.

Brighouse, T. and Woods, D.C. (2006) *Inspirations.* London: Network Continuum Education.

Broderick, P.C. and Metz, S. (2009) 'Learning to BREATHE: A pilot trial of a mindfulness curriculum for adolescents'. *Advances in School Mental Health Promotion*, 2 (1), 35–46. DOI:10.1080/1754730X.2009.9715696.

Brown, G. and Coles, M. (2014) 'Our children should know themselves: Schools and the black child, new conversations'. *Race Equality Teaching*, 32 (2), 31–5.

Burke, C.A. (2010) 'Mindfulness-based approaches with children and adolescents: A preliminary review of current research in an emergent field'. *Journal of Child and Family Studies*, 19 (2), 133–44.

Buzan, T. (2001) *The Power of Spiritual Intelligence: 10 ways to tap into your spiritual genius:* London: Thorsons.

Cameron, D. (2011) 'PM calls for "shared national identity"'. Prime Minister's Office. Online. www.gov.uk/government/news/pm-calls-for-shared-national-identity (accessed June 2015).

Cantle, T. (n.d.) *Community Cohesion: A Report of the Independent Review Team.* London: Home Office. Online. http://dera.ioe.ac.uk/14146/1/communitycohesionreport.pdf (accessed June 2015).

Cantle, T. (2012) *Interculturalism: The new era of cohesion and diversity.* Basingstoke: Palgrave Macmillan.

Carlson, L.E. (2012) 'Mindfulness-Based Interventions for Physical Conditions: A Narrative Review Evaluating Levels of Evidence'. *ISRN Psychiatry*, 2012.

Carlson, L.E., Speca, M., Faris, P. and Patel, K.D. (2007) 'One year pre-post intervention follow-up of psychological, immune, endocrine and blood pressure outcomes of mindfulness-based stress reduction (MBSR) in breast and prostate cancer outpatients'. *Brain, Behavior, and Immunity*, 21, 1038–49.

Carmody, J. and Baer, R.A. (2008) 'Relationships between mindfulness practice and levels of mindfulness, medical and psychological symptoms and well-being in a mindfulness-based stress reduction program'. *Journal of Behavioral Medicine*, 31 (1), 23–33.

Cayton, P. (2011) *Compassion in Education: An introduction to creating compassionate cultures*. London: Foundation for Developing Wisdom and Compassion.

Chang, L. (2006) *Wisdom for the Soul*, India: Embassy Books.

Chiesa, A. and Serretti, A. (2009) 'Mindfulness-based stress reduction for stress management in healthy people: A review and metaanalysis. *Journal of Alternative and Complementary Medicine*, 15, 593–600.

Childhood Wellbeing Research Centre (2012) *The Impact of Pupil Behaviour and Wellbeing on Educational Outcomes*. DFE-RR253. London: Department for Education.

City of Birmingham Education Department (1985) *Education for Our Multicultural Society*. Online. www.coedfoundation.org.uk (accessed July 2014).

Cohen-Katz, J., Wiley, S.D., Capuano, T., Baker, D.M. and Shapiro, S. (2004) 'The effects of mindfulness-based stress reduction on nurse stress and burnout: A quantitative and qualitative study'. *Holistic Nursing Practice*, 18 (6), 302–8.

Coles, M.I. (ed.) (2007) *Faith, Interfaith and Cohesion: The education dimension*. Online. www.coedfoundation.org.uk/pdfs/Interfaith_Project.pdf (accessed January 2015).

Coles, M. and Scoble, F. (2012) The Sacred Spaces Project. February. Online. www.coedfoundation.org.uk/pdfs/The%20Sacred%20Spaces%20Project.pdf (accessed June 2014).

Creswell, J.D., Irwin, M.R., Burklund, L.J., Lieberman, M.D., Arevalo, J.M.G., Ma, J., Crabb Breen, E., Cole, S.W. (2012) 'Mindfulness-Based Stress Reduction training reduces loneliness and pro-inflammatory gene expression in older adults: A small randomized controlled trial'. *Brain, Behavior, and Immunity*, 26 (7), 1095–101.

Cruttwell, A. (2012) *Shropshire Respect Yourself Improving Relationships and Sex Education (RSE) Programme 6–11*. Shropshire Council.

Cusens, B., Duggan, G.B., Thorne, K. and Burch, V. (2010) 'Evaluation of the breathworks mindfulness-based pain management programme: Effects on well-being and multiple measures of mindfulness'. *Clinical Psychology and Psychotherapy*, 17 (1), 63–78.

Cush, D. (2011) 'Championing the Underdog: a Positive Pluralist Approach to Religious Education for Equality and Diversity'. Ph.D. diss., University of Warwick.

Dalai Lama with Chan, V. (2012) *The Wisdom of Compassion*. London: Bantam Press

Dalton, J. and Fairchild, L. (2004) *The Compassionate Classroom: Lessons that nurture wisdom and empathy*. Chicago: Zephyr Press.

Davidson, R.J., Kabat-Zinn, J., Schumacher, J., Rosenkranz, M., Muller, D., Santorelli, S.F., Urbanowski, F., Harrington, A., Bonus, K. and Sheridan, J.F. (2003) 'Alterations in brain and immune function produced by mindfulness meditation'. *Psychosomatic Medicine*, 65 (4), 564–70.

DCSF (2007) *Every Child Matters: Duty to promote the wellbeing of pupils at the school. Section 38 (1) Education and Inspections Act*. London: Department for Children, Schools and Families.

De Chardin, P.T. (1955) *The Phenomenon of Man*. London: William Collins Sons and Co.

Dewar, B. and Christley, Y. (2013) 'A critical analysis of Compassion in Practice'. *Nursing Standard*, 28 (10), 46–50.

DfE (2010a) *Social and Emotional Aspects of Learning (SEAL) Programme in Secondary Schools: National evaluation*. London: Department for Education. Online. www.gov.uk/government/publications/social-and-emotional-aspects-of-learning-seal-programme-in-secondary-schools-national-evaluation (accessed May 2015).

DfE (2010b) *The Importance of Teaching: The Schools White Paper on Education*. London: Department for Education. Online. www.gov.uk/government/uploads/system/uploads/attachment_data/file/175429/CM-7980.pdf (accessed June 2015).

DfE (2013a) *The National Curriculum in England. Key stages 1 and 2 framework document*. London: Department for Education. Online. www.gov.uk/government/uploads/system/uploads/attachment_data/file/425601/PRIMARY_national_curriculum.pdf (accessed June 2015).

DfE (2013b) *Consultation on PSHE Education: Summary report*. London: Department for Education. Online. http://media.education.gov.uk/assets/files/pdf/p/pshe%20cons%20report.pdf (accessed June 2015).

DfE (2013c) *Reforming the National Curriculum in England: Summary report of the July to August 2013 consultation on the new programmes of study and attainment targets from September 2014*. London: Department for Education. Online. www.gov.uk/government/uploads/system/uploads/attachment_data/file/239270/Consultation_Summary_Response_NC_v3.pdf (accessed June 2015).

DfE (2014a) *The National Curriculum in England. Key stages 3 and 4 framework document*. London: Department for Education. Online. www.gov.uk/government/uploads/system/uploads/attachment_data/file/381754/SECONDARY_national_curriculum.pdf (accessed June 2015).

DfE (2014b) *The National Curriculum in England. Framework document*. London: Department for Education. Online. www.gov.uk/government/uploads/system/uploads/attachment_data/file/335116/Master_final_national_curriculum_220714.pdf (accessed June 2015).

DH (2005) *National Healthy School Status: A guide for schools*. London: Department of Health.

DH (2010) *Healthy Lives, Healthy People: Our strategy for public health in England*. London: Department of Health. Online. www.gov.uk/government/uploads/system/uploads/attachment_data/file/216096/dh_127424.pdf (accessed June 2015).

DH (2012) *Better Health Outcomes for Children and Young People: Our pledge.* London: Department of Health.

DH (2013) *Improving Children and Young People's Health Outcomes: A systems wide response.* London: Department of Health.

Dossey, L. (2013) *One Mind.* London: Hayhouse.

Eaude, T. (2008) *Children's Spiritual, Moral, Social and Cultural Development: Primary and Early Years.* Exeter: Sage.

Eberth, J. and Sedlmeier, P. (2012) 'The effects of mindfulness meditation: A meta-analysis'. *Mindfulness*, 3 (3), 174–89.

EC (European Community) (1989) *Resolution of the Council of Ministers of Education meeting within Council 23rd November 1988, concerning health education and schools (89/C/S/01).* Official Journal of the European Commission.

Eccles, J.S. and Roeser, R.W. (2009) 'Schools, academic motivation, and stage-environment fit'. In Lerner, R.M. and Steinberg, L.D. (eds) *Handbook of Adolescent Psychology.* 3rd ed. Hoboken, N.J.: John Wiley & Sons, Inc.

Ekman, P. (2014) *Moving Toward Global compassion,* San Francisco: Paul Ekman Group.

Engström, M. and Söderfeldt, B. (2010) 'Brain activation during compassion meditation: A case study'. *The Journal of Alternative and Complementary Medicine*, 16 (5), 597–9.

Foresight (2013) *Future Identities: Changing identities in the UK – the next 10 years.* Government Office for Science. Online. www.gov.uk/government/uploads/system/uploads/attachment_data/file/273966/13-523-future-identities-changing-identities-report.pdf (accessed June 2015).

Francis, L.J. and Robbins, M. (2005) *Urban Hope and Spiritual Health: The Adolescent Voice.* Werrington, Peterborough: Epworth Press.

Frank, J.L., Jennings, P.A. and Greenberg, M.T. (2013) 'Mindfulness-based interventions in school settings: An introduction to the Special Issue'. *Research in Human Development*, 10 (3), 205–10.

Fromm, E. (1957) *The Art of Loving.* St Ives: Thorsons.

Fryer, B. (2013) 'The rise of compassionate management (finally)'. *Harvard Business Review*. Online. https://hbr.org/2013/09/the-rise-of-compassionate-management-finally/ (accessed December 2014).

Fullan, M. (2001) *Leading in a Culture of Change.* San Francisco: Jossey-Bass.

Gardner, H. (1983) *Frames of Mind: The theory of multiple intelligences.* New York: Basic Books.

Germer, C. K. (2009) *The Mindful Path to Self-compassion: Freeing yourself from destructive thoughts and emotions.* New York: Guilford Press.

Gilbert, P. (2010a) *Compassion Focused Therapy: Distinctive features.* 1st ed. London; New York: Routledge.

Gilbert, P. (2010b) *The Compassionate Mind.* Re-issue. London: Constable.

Gilbert, P. and Procter, S. (2006) 'Compassionate mind training for people with high shame and self-criticism: Overview and pilot study of a group therapy approach'. *Clinical Psychology and Psychotherapy*, 13 (6), 353–79.

Gillborn, D. (2008) *Racism and Education: Coincidence or conspiracy?* Abingdon, Oxon: Routledge.

Goetz, J.L., Keltner, D. and Simon-Thomas, E. (2010) 'Compassion: An evolutionary analysis and empirical review'. *Psychological Bulletin*, 136 (3), 351–74.

Goldenberg, S. (2013) 'Climate change included in US science teaching guidelines for the first time'. *The Guardian*, 9 April. Online. www.theguardian.com/environment/2013/apr/09/climate-change-us-science-teaching (accessed June 2015).

Goleman, D. (1996) *Emotional Intelligence: Why it can matter more than IQ*. London: Bloomsbury.

Goodman, A. and Gregg, P. (2010) *The Importance of Attitudes and Behaviour for Poorer Children's Educational Attainment*. London: Joseph Rowntree Foundation.

Gordon, M. (2009) *Roots of Empathy: Changing the world child by child*. New York: Experiment.

Grepmair, L., Mitterlehner, F., Loew, T., Bachler, E., Rother, W. and Nickel, M. (2007) 'Promoting mindfulness in psychotherapists in training influences the treatment results of their patients: A randomized, double-blind, controlled study'. *Psychotherapy and Psychosomatics*, 76 (6), 332–8.

Grossman, P., Niemann, L., Schmidt, S. and Walach, H. (2004) 'Mindfulness-based stress reduction and health benefits. A meta-analysis'. *Journal of Psychosomatic Research*, 57 (1), 35–43.

The Guardian (2014) *Loving languages*. Special report. 14 October. Online. www.pressreader.com/uk/loving-language (accessed June 2015).

Hann, M. (2015) 'Pharrell Williams and Al Gore announce Live Earth 2015'. *The Guardian*, 21 January. Online. www.theguardian.com/music/2015/jan/21/pharrell-williams-announces-live-earth-2015-davos (accessed February 2015).

Hanson, R., with Mendius, R. (2009) *Buddha's Brain*. Oakland: New Harbinger Publications Inc.

Harrison, N., James, D. and Last, K. (2012) *The impact of the pursuit of ASDAN's Certificate of Personal Effectiveness (CoPE) on GCSE Attainment*. Bristol: ASDAN/University of the West of England. Online. www.asdan.org.uk/news/2014-04-report-shows-cope-boosts-pupils-gcse-success (accessed June 2015).

Hart, S. and Kindle Hodson, V. (2004) *The Compassionate Classroom: Relationship-based teaching and learning*. Encinitas, CA: PuddleDancer Press.

Hattie, J. and Yates, G. (2013) *Visible Learning and the Science of How We Learn*. Oxford: Routledge.

Havel, V. (1992) *Summer Meditations*. Essay cited in Montgomery, P. (2012) 'Democracy as spiritual discipline'. *Religion Dispatches*. Online. http://religiondispatches.org/vaclav-havel-democracy-as-spiritual-discipline (accessed June 2015).

Hawkes, N. (2013) *From My Heart: Transforming lives through values*. Carmarthen: Independent Thinking Press.

Hay, D., with Nye, R. (2006) *The Spirit of the Child*. London: Jessica Kingsley Publishers.

Hodge, S. (2011) *Charting a Health Literacy Journey*. London: Royal Society for Public Health.

Holzel, B.K., Lazar, S.W., Gard, T., Schuman-Olivier, Z., Vago, D.R. and Ott, U. (2011) 'How Does Mindfulness Meditation Work? Proposing Mechanisms of Action From a Conceptual and Neural Perspective'. *Perspectives on Psychological Science*, 6 (6), 537–59.

Holzel, B.K., Ott, U., Gard, T., Hempel, H., Weygandt, M., Morgen, K. and Vaitl, D. (2007) 'Investigation of mindfulness meditation practitioners with voxel-based morphometry'. *Social Cognitive and Affective Neuroscience*, 3 (1), 55–61.

HSCIC (2014) *National Child Measurement Programme – England, 2013–14*. Online. www.hscic.gov.uk/searchcatalogue?productid=16565&q=obesity&sort=Relevance&size=10&page=1#top (accessed June 2015).

Huppert, F.A. and Johnson, D.M. (2010) 'A controlled trial of mindfulness training in schools: The importance of practice for an impact on well-being'. *The Journal of Positive Psychology*, 5 (4), 264–74.

IMF (2015) *Causes and Consequences of Income Inequality: A global perspective*. Online. www.imf.org/external/pubs/ft/sdn/2015/sdn1513.pdf (accessed September 2015).

Immordino-Yang, M.H., McColl, A., Damasio, H. and Damasio, A. (2009) 'Neural correlates of admiration and compassion'. *Proceedings of the National Academy of Sciences*, 106 (19), 8021–6. pnas.0810363106.

Insted (2014) 'Questioning the Trojan Horse: Some key articles'. Online. www.insted.co.uk/questioning-trojan-horse.pdf (accessed June 2015).

IPCC (2014) *Fifth Assessment Report*. Online. www.ipcc.ch (accessed February 2015).

Jacobsen, P., Morris, E., Johns, L. and Hodkinson, K. (2011) 'Mindfulness Groups for Psychosis; Key Issues for Implementation on an Inpatient Unit'. *Behavioural and Cognitive Psychotherapy*, 39 (3), 349–53.

Jazaieri, H., McGonigal, K., Jinpa, T., Doty, J.R., Gross, J.J. and Goldin, P.R. (2014) 'A randomized controlled trial of compassion cultivation training: Effects on mindfulness, affect, and emotion regulation'. *Motivation and Emotion*, 38 (1), 23–35.

Johnson, A.O. and Neagley, W.N. (2011) *Educating from the Heart*. New York: Rowman and Littlefield.

Joyce, A., Etty-Leal, J., Zazryn, T. and Hamilton, A. (2010) 'Exploring a mindfulness meditation program on the mental health of upper primary children: A pilot study'. *Advances in School Mental Health Promotion*, 3 (2), 17–25.

Jubilee Centre for Character and Virtues (2013) *A Framework for Character Education in Schools*. University of Birmingham pamphlet. Online. http://jubileecentre.ac.uk/userfiles/jubileecentre/pdf/other-centre-papers/Framework.pdf (accessed June 2015).

Kabat-Zinn, J. (1982) 'An outpatient program in behavioral medicine for chronic pain patients based on the practice of mindfulness meditation: Theoretical considerations and preliminary results'. *General Hospital Psychiatry*, 4 (1), 33–47.

Khoury, B., Lecomte, T., Fortin, G., Masse, M., Therien, P., Bouchard, V., Chapleau, M.A., Paquin, K. and Hofmann, S.G. (2013) 'Mindfulness-based therapy: A comprehensive meta-analysis'. *Clinical Psychology Review*, 33 (6), 763–71. doi:10.1016/j.cpr.2013.05.005.

Kickbusch, I. (2008) 'Health literacy: An essential skill for the 21st century'. *Health Education*, 108 (2), 1011–104.

Kickbusch, I., Wait, S. and Maag, D. (2006) *Navigating Health, the Role of Health Literacy*. London: Alliance for Health and the Future.

King, Martin Luther, Jr (1963) *Strength to Love*. New York: Harper and Row.

King, Martin Luther, Jr (1964a) 'The Nobel Peace Prize 1964 Acceptance Speech'. Online. www.nobelprize.org/nobel_prizes/peace/laureates/1964/king-acceptance. html (accessed June 2015).

King, Martin Luther, Jr (1964b) 'A Mighty Army of Love'. *SCLC Newsletter* 2, Oct/Nov. Atlanta, Ga.: Southern Christian Leadership Conference.

Klimecki, O.M., Leiberg, S., Lamm, C. and Singer, T. (2013) 'Functional neural plasticity and associated changes in positive affect after compassion training'. *Cerebral Cortex*, 23 (7), 1552–61. DOI:10.1093/cercor/bhs142.

Klimecki, O.M., Leiberg, S., Ricard, M. and Singer, T. (2014) 'Differential pattern of functional brain plasticity after compassion and empathy training'. *Social Cognitive and Affective Neuroscience*, 9 (6), 873–9.

Krznaric, R. (2014) *Empathy: A handbook for revolution*. London: Rider Books.

Kuyken, W., Watkins, E., Holden, E., White, K., Taylor, R.S., Byford, S. and Dalgleish, T. (2010) 'How does mindfulness-based cognitive therapy work?' *Behaviour Research and Therapy*, 48 (11), 1105–12.

Kuyken, W., Weare, K., Ukoumunne, O.C., Vicary, R., Motton, N., Burnett, R. and Huppert, F. (2013) 'Effectiveness of the Mindfulness in Schools Programme: Non-randomised controlled feasibility study'. *The British Journal of Psychiatry: The Journal of Mental Science*, 203 (2), 126–31.

Laloux, F. (2014) *Reinventing Organizations: A guide to creating organizations inspired by the next stage of human consciousness*. Brussels: Nelson Parker.

Lavian, R.H. (2012) 'The impact of organizational climate on burnout among homeroom teachers and special education teachers (full classes/individual pupils) in mainstream schools'. *Teachers and Teaching*, 18 (2), 233–47.

Layard, R. (2009) *A Good Childhood: Searching for values in a competitive age*. London: Penguin Books.

— (2011) *Happiness: Lessons from a new science*. London: Penguin Books.

Lazar, S.W., Kerr, C.E., Wasserman, R.H., Gray, J.R., Greve, D.N., Treadway, M.T., McGarvey, M., Quinn, B.T., Dusek, J.A., Benson, H., Rauch, S.L., Moore, C.I. and Fischl, B. (2005) 'Meditation experience is associated with increased cortical thickness'. *Neuroreport*, 16 (17), 1893–7.

Lewis, C.S (1961) *An Experiment in Criticism*. Cambridge: Cambridge University Press. Kindle edition.

Lewis, H.R. (2006) *Excellence Without A Soul*. New York: Public Affairs.

Lloyd, J. (2013) 'Improving health outcomes and health literacy for children and young people through Personal, Social and Health education in schools'. Paper presented at the 17th EUSUHM Congress, London: Royal College of General Practitioners, 27 June.

London Challenge (n.d.) *10x16 Pledge Planner. The London Student Pledge: 10 things to do by the time you're 16*. Online. http://webarchive.nationalarchives. gov.uk/20070108123845/http:/dfes.gov.uk/londonchallenge/pdfs/Pledge%20 Planner%2026%5B1%5D.01.05%20.pdf (accessed January 2015).

Lucas, B. (2009) *rEvolution: How to thrive in crazy times*. Carmarthen: Crown House Publishing.

Luders, E., Kurth, F., Mayer, E.A., Toga, A.W., Narr, K.L. and Gaser, C. (2012) 'The unique brain anatomy of meditation practitioners: Alterations in cortical gyrification'. *Frontiers in Human Neuroscience*, 6.

Lutz, A., Brefczynski-Lewis, J., Johnstone, T. and Davidson, R.J. (2008) 'Regulation of the neural circuitry of emotion by compassion meditation: Effects of meditative expertise'. *PLoS ONE*, 3 (3), e1897.

Lynch, S., Styles. B., Dawson, A., Worth, J., Kerr, D. and Lloyd, J. (2013) *Talk About Alcohol: an Evaluation of the Alcohol Education Trust's Intervention in Secondary Schools*. Slough: National Foundation for Educational Research.

Macdonald, A. (2009) *Independent review of the proposals to make Personal, Social, Health and Economic (PSHE) education statutory*. London: Department for Children, Schools and Families.

Mackey-Kallis, S. (2001) *The Hero and the Perennial Journey Home in American Film*, Philadelphia: University of Pennsylvania Press.

McLaughlin, C. with Davidson, G. (2010) *The Practical Visionary: A new world guide to spiritual growth and change*. Unity.

Macpherson, W. *The Stephen Lawrence Inquiry Report* (1999). Online. https://www.gov.uk/government/uploads/system/uploads/attachment_data/file/277111/4262.pdf (accessed June 2015).

McWhirter, J.M. (2014) 'The draw and write technique as a versatile tool for researching children's understanding of health and well–being'. *International Journal of Health Promotion and Education (IJHPE)*, 52 (5–6), 250–60.

Marmot, M. *et al.* (2010) *Fair Society, Healthy Lives. The Marmot Review: Strategic review of health inequalities in England post-2010*. Online. www.instituteofhealthequity.org/projects/fair-society-healthy-lives-the-marmot-review (accessed June 2015).

Maslow, A. (1954) *Motivation and Personality*. New York: Harper & Row.

— (1964) *Religions, Values, and Peak-experiences*. Columbus: Ohio State University Press.

Mitra, S. (2013) *School in the Cloud*. Online. www.ted.com/talks/sugata_mitra_build_a_school_in_the_cloud?language=en (accessed February 2014).

Monbiot, G. (2013) 'Materialism: a system that eats us from the inside out'. *The Guardian*, 9 December. Online. www.theguardian.com/commentisfree/2013/dec/09/materialism-system-eats-us-from-inside-out (accessed July 2014).

Murdoch, A. and Oldershaw, D. (2009) *16 Guidelines for a Happy Life*. London: Foundation for Developing Compassion and Wisdom.

Murphy, M.J., Mermelstein, L.C., Edwards, K.M. and Gidycz, C.A. (2012) 'The benefits of dispositional mindfulness in physical health: A longitudinal study of female college students'. *Journal of American College Health*, 60 (5), 341–8.

Murphy-Paul, Annie (2015) *Brilliant: The new science of smart*. New York: Random House.

NACCCE (1999) *All Our Futures: Creativity, culture and education*. Online. http://sirkenrobinson.com/pdf/allourfutures.pdf (accessed October 2014).

NatCen (2014) 'Brits just as racially prejudiced as a decade ago'. Press release *NatCen*, 27 May. Online. www.natcen.ac.uk/news-media/press-releases/2014/may/brits-just-as-racially-prejudiced-as-30-years-ago/ (accessed June 2015).

NCC (1990) *Curriculum Guidance 5. Health Education*. York: National Curriculum Council.

Neff, K. (2011) *Self-Compassion: The proven power of being kind to yourself*. New York: William Morrow.

Neff, K.D. and Germer, C.K. (2013) 'A pilot study and randomized controlled trial of the mindful self-compassion program'. *Journal of Clinical Psychology*, 69 (1), 28–44.

Neff, K.D., Hsieh, Y.-P. and Dejitterat, K. (2005) 'Self-compassion, achievement goals, and coping with academic failure'. *Self and Identity*, 4 (3), 263–87.

Nesbitt, E. (2004) *Intercultural Education, Ethnographic and Religious Approach*. Sussex: Sussex Academic Press.

Newton, J. (2013) Key note address, presented at the 17th EUSUHM Congress, London: Royal College of General Practitioners. 27 June.

Ng, Pak Tee (2014) 'Singapore: Teach Less, Learn More'. The Brainwaves Video Anthology, 23 September. *YouTube*. Online. www.youtube.com/watch?v=lnuGwhIZJhI.

NICE (2013) 'Social and emotional wellbeing for children and young people'. NICE Local Government Briefing 12. London: National Institute for Health and Care Excellence. Online. http://nice.org.uk/lgb12 (accessed June 2015).

Nutbeam, D. (2008) 'Evolving concept of health literacy'. *Social Science and Medicine*, 67, 2072–8.

Ofsted (2004) *Promoting and evaluating pupils' spiritual, moral, social and cultural development*. HMI 2125. Online. http://dera.ioe.ac.uk/4959/ (accessed June 2015).

Ofsted (2013) *Not Yet Good Enough: Personal, social and health education in English Schools in 2012*. London: Office for Standards in Education.

Orr, D. (1994) *Earth in Mind*. Washington: Island Press.

Oxfam (2014) 'Report out today shows the UK's five richest families are wealthier than the poorest 20% of the population combined'. *Oxfam*. Blog, 17 March. Online. http://www.oxfam.org.uk/blogs/2014/03/5-richest-families-in-uk-are-wealthier-than-poorest-20-pc.

Oztop, E., Kawato, M. and Arbib, M.A. (2013) 'Mirror neurons: Functions, mechanisms and models'. *Neuroscience Letters*, 540, 43–55.

Parekh, B. (2000) *The Future of Multi-ethnic Britain* (the 'Parekh Report'). London: Profile Books.

Peters, T. and Waterman, R.H. (1982) *In Search Of Excellence: Lessons from America's best-run companies*. New York: HarperCollins.

Peterson, A., Lexmond, T., Hallgarten, T. and Kerr, D. (2014) *Schools with Soul: A new approach to spiritual, moral, social and cultural education*. Online. www.thersa.org/discover/publications-and-articles/reports/schools-with-soul-a-new-approach-to-spiritual-moral-social-and-cultural-education/ (accessed September 2014).

Piketty, T. (2014) *Capital in the Twenty-First Century*. Trans. Goldhammer, A. Cambridge, MA: Harvard University Press.

PHE (2014) *The Link Between Pupil Health and Well-being and Attainment: A briefing for headteachers, governors and staff in education settings*. London: Public Health England. Online. www.gov.uk/government/publications/the-link-between-pupil-health-and-wellbeing-and-attainment (accessed June 2015).

PSHE Association (2013) 'Ten Principles of PSHE Education'. Online. www.pshe-association.org.uk (accessed June 2015).

QCA (1997) *The Promotion of Pupils' Spiritual, Moral, Social and Cultural Development: Draft guidance for pilot work*. London: Qualifications and Curriculum Authority.

QCA (1998) *Education for Citizenship and the Teaching of Democracy in Schools*. Final report of the Advisory Group on Citizenship, chairman Crick, B. London: QCA.

QCA (2007) *The National Curriculum Statutory Requirements for Key Stages 3 and 4*. London: QCA.

Rawle, D.M. (2011) 'Perceptions of Spirituality and Spiritual Development in Education held by Teachers and Students on Teacher Training Courses'. PhD diss., UWIC.

Redfield, J. (1993) *The Celestine Prophecy*. New York: Time Warner.

Redfield, J. (1997) *The Celestine Vision*. London: Bantam.

Rees, G., Francis, L.J. and Robbins, M. (2005) *Spiritual Health and the Well-Being of Urban Young People*. The Commission on Urban Life and Faith/University of Wales/The Children's Society.

Richardson, R. and Bolloten, B. (2014) 'Fundamental British values – origins, controversy, ways forward: A symposium'. *Race Equality Teaching* 32(3).

Robinson, K. (2014) 'Sir Ken Robinson criticises Pisa for being "too narrow"'. *TES*. 27 March. Online. https://www.tes.co.uk/news/school-news/breaking-news/sir-ken-robinson-criticises-pisa-being-too-narrow (accessed June 2015).

Robinson, K. and Aronica, L. (2013) *Finding your Element: How to discover your talents and passions and transform your life*. London: Penguin Books.

Roeser, R.W., Schonert-Reichl, K.A., Jha, A., Cullen, M., Wallace, L., Wilensky, R., Oberle, E., Thomson, K., Taylor, C. and Harrison, J. (2013) 'Mindfulness training and reductions in teacher stress and burnout: Results from two randomized, waitlist-control field trials'. *Journal of Educational Psychology*, 105 (3), 787–804.

Rotne, K. and Rotne, D.F. (2013) *Everybody Present: Mindfulness in Education*. Berkeley, California: Parallax Press.

RSA (Royal Society of Arts) (2014) *RSA Journal*, 2 (special issue: *The Power to Create*). Online. www.thersa.org/discover/publications-and-articles/journals/issue-2-2014 (accessed May 2015).

Runnymede Trust (2003) *Complementing Teachers: A practical guide to promoting race equality in schools*. Online. http://open.tean.ac.uk/handle/123456789/605 (accessed July 2014).

Russell, T.A. (2011) 'Body in mind training: Mindful movement for severe and enduring mental illness'. *British Journal of Wellbeing*, 2 (4), 13–16.

Russell, T.A. (2014) 'Body in Mind? The need for an integrative approach to compassion in the NHS'. *Journal of Holistic Healthcare*, 11 (1), 7–10.

Russell, T. and Tatton-Ramos, T. (2014) 'Body in mind training: Mindful movement for the clinical setting'. *Neuro-Disability and Psychotherapy: A Forum for the Practice and Development of Psychological Therapies for Neurological Conditions*, 2 (1), 108–36.

Schonert-Reichl, K.A. and Lawlor, M.S. (2010) 'The effects of a mindfulness-based education program on pre- and early adolescents' well-being and social and emotional competence'. *Mindfulness*, 1 (3), 137–51.

Schonert-Reichl, K.A., Oberle, E., Lawlor, M.S., Abbott, D., Thomson, K., Oberlander, T.F. and Diamond, A., n.d. *Enhancing Cognitive and Social-Emotional Development Through a Simple-to-Administer School Program*. MS. Online. http://discovermindfulness.ca/wp-content/uploads/2013/08/Schonert-Reichl-et-al.-MindUp-RCT-2012-Under-Review.pdf (accessed June 2015).

Shapiro, S.L., Brown, K.W. and Biegel, G.M. (2007) 'Teaching selfcare to caregivers: Effects of Mindfulness-Based Stress Reduction on the mental health of therapists in training'. *Training and Education in Professional Psychology*, 1, 105–15.

Shapiro, S.L., Carlson, L.E., Astin, J.A. and Freedman, B. (2006) 'Mechanisms of mindfulness'. *Journal of Clinical Psychology*, 62 (3), 373–86.

Sihota, S. and Lennard, L. (2004) *Health Literacy: Being able to make the most of health*. London: National Consumer Council.

Spencer, E., Lucas, B. and Claxton, G. (2012) *Progression in Creativity*. Online. www.creativitycultureeducation.org/wp-content/uploads/Progression-in-Creativity-Final-Report-April-2012.pdf (accessed November 2014).

Stanley, T. (2013) 'Sorry, Boris Johnson: greed is neither good nor conservative'. *The Telegraph*. 29 November. Online. http://blogs.telegraph.co.uk/news/timstanley/100248300/sorry-boris-johnson-greed-is-neither-good-nor-conservative (accessed February 2015).

Stewart, W. (2013) 'How Pisa came to rule the world'. *TES*. Online. www.tes.co.uk/article.aspx?storyCode=6379193 (accessed December 2014).

Stoll, L., Fink, D. and Earl, L. (2003) *It's About Learning (and It's About Time): What's in it for schools?* London: Routledge Falmer.

Sutton Trust and Education Endowment Foundation (2013) *Teaching and Learning Toolkit*. EEF. Online. https://educationendowmentfoundation.org.uk/uploads/toolkit/Teaching_and_Learning_Toolkit_(Spring_2013).pdf.

Sze, J.A., Gyurak, A., Yuan, J.W. and Levenson, R.W. (2010) 'Coherence between emotional experience and physiology: Does body awareness training have an impact?' *Emotion* (Washington, D.C.), 10 (6), 803–14.

Teasdale, W., with a Foreword by the Dalai Lama (1999) *The Mystic Heart*. Novato: New World Library.

Temple Guy (2004) Online. http://thetempleguy.com/articles/mail/trans-2-trans.htm (accessed January 2015).

Thera, N. (2013) 'The Practice of Loving-Kindness (Metta): As Taught by the Buddha in the Pali Canon'. Online. *Access to Insight* (Legacy Edition), 30 November 2013. www.accesstoinsight.org/lib/authors/nanamoli/wheel007.html (accessed January 2014).

Thompson, M. and Gauntlett-Gilbert, J. (2008) 'Mindfulness with children and adolescents: Effective clinical application'. *Clinical Child Psychology and Psychiatry*, 13 (3), 395–407.

UNICEF (1989) *United Nations Convention on the Rights of the Child*. Online. www.unicef.org.uk/Documents/Publication-pdfs/UNCRC_PRESS200910web.pdf (accessed June 2015).

Van Dam, N.T., Sheppard, S.C., Forsyth, J.P. and Earleywine, M. (2011) 'Self-compassion is a better predictor than mindfulness of symptom severity and quality of life in mixed anxiety and depression'. *Journal of Anxiety Disorders*, 25 (1), 123–30.

Vaughan-Lee, E. (n.d.(a)) *One: The Project*. Online. http://onetheproject.com (accessed June 2015).

Vaughan-Lee, E. (n.d.(b)) 'Elemental the film'. *Facebook*. Online. www.facebook.com/elementalfilm (accessed June 2015).

Vaughan-Lee, L. (ed.) (2002) *Working with Oneness*. California: Golden Sufi Center Publishing.

— (2013a) 'Changing the Story'. Blog, *Huffington Post*. Online. www.huffingtonpost.com/llewellyn-vaughanlee/changing-the-story_b_2681252.html (accessed June 2015).

— (2013b) *Spiritual Ecology: The cry of the Earth*. California: Golden Sufi Center Publishing.

Wallace, B.A. and Goleman, D. (2006) *The Attention Revolution: Unlocking the power of the focused mind*. Boston: Wisdom Publications.

Waters, M. (2013) *Thinking Allowed on Schooling*. Carmarthen: Independent Thinking Press.

White, L.S. (2012) 'Reducing stress in school-age girls through mindful yoga'. *Journal of Pediatric Health Care: Official Publication of National Association of Pediatric Nurse Associates & Practitioners*, 26 (1), 45–56.

Wilkinson, R. and Pickett, K. (2010) *The Spirit Level: Why Equality is Better for Everyone*. London: Penguin.

Williams, J.M.G. and Penman, D. (2012) *Mindfulness: An eight-week plan for finding peace in a frantic world*. [Emmaus, Pa.]: Rodale Books.

Wood, S. and Higgins, D. (2011) 'Integrating the spirit with total body fitness'. In Johnson, A.O. and Neagley, W.N. *Educating from the Heart*. New York: Rowman and Littlefield.

Woodruff, S.C., Glass, C.R., Arnkoff, D.B., Crowley, K.J., Hindman, R.K. and Hirschhorn, E.W. (2013) 'Comparing self-compassion, mindfulness, and psychological inflexibility as predictors of psychological health'. *Mindfulness*, 1–12.

Yacoboni, C. (2014) *How Do You Pray?* New York: Monkfish.

Zabel, R.H. and Zabel, M.K. (2001) 'Revisiting burnout among special education teachers: Do age, experience, and preparation still matter?' *Teacher Education and Special Education: The Journal of the Teacher Education Division of the Council for Exceptional Children*, 24, 128–39.

Zeusse, E. (2013) 'United States Is Now the Most Unequal of All Advanced Economies'. *Huffington Post*, 8 December. Online. www.huffingtonpost.com/eric-zuesse/us-is-now-the-most-unequal_b_4408647.html (accessed December 2014).

Zinger, L. (2011) 'Educating for tolerance and compassion: Is there a place for meditation in a college classroom? *College Teaching Methods & Styles Journal (CTMS)*, 4 (4), 25–8.

Zohar, D. and Marshall, I. (2000) *SQ: Spiritual Intelligence, the ultimate intelligence*. London: Bloomsbury.

Index

Index